Paul, Mandy, Alexander and William, pictured at Christmas 1989 just three weeks before the collapse of Chancery Bank. A happy young family with the world at their feet. Mandy is heavily pregnant with their youngest son Harrison – Harrison is to be born on March 7th 1990, a few weeks after the crash of the bank.

Today, Paul and Mandy live happily in his beloved Fens of Cambridgeshire in the very same thatched home, in the same pony-paddocked grounds where they originally lived!

Attacked and Left for Dead is their true story!

Following the true events contained in this book, amazingly, Paul got back on his feet and from absolutely nothing he went on to make his second self-made multi-million pound fortune.

To discover how he did this, you must read his next new forthcoming novel, *From Zero To Hero!*

ATTACKED AND LEFT FOR DEAD

Warning: This book is not fiction, it is fact!

In 2012 billions of innocent people throughout the world are in extremely serious danger right now!

Because as the law stands today, when a bank goes bust, *no government anywhere in the world* is forced by law to give 100% protection or pay out 100% compensation to the innocent!

So if you have savings or borrowings, no matter how small or how big you think, you are, you are definitely in very serious trouble!

With the exception of a few names that I have changed, the circumstances detailed in this disturbing and shocking book are all true!

Paul G Salter

Paul G Salter

ATTACKED AND LEFT FOR DEAD

Vanguard Press

VANGUARD PAPERBACK

© Copyright 2012
Paul G Salter

The right of Paul G Salter to be identified as author of
this work has been asserted by him in accordance with the
Copyright, Designs and Patents Act 1988.

A CIP catalogue record for this title is
available from the British Library.

ISBN 978 1 84386 837 8

Vanguard Press is an imprint of
Pegasus Elliot MacKenzie Publishers Ltd.
www.pegasuspublishers.com

First Published in 2012

Vanguard Press
Sheraton House Castle Park
Cambridge England

Printed & Bound in Great Britain

Disclaimer

The opinion of the behaviour of the characters contained in this book are the personal views and beliefs of the author, particularly to the non action of the Thatcher Government to come to the rescue of the completely innocent customers of the collapsed three London banks and the aggressive, relentless and very hostile action of the receivers to the collapsed Chancery Bank of London.

I dedicate this book to my wife Mandy: my everything, who through all the pain kept me sane.

Today as you read this true astonishing, frank and brutal book, you run the very real risk that you will lose your life savings, your home and everything else that you possess too, because the bank that you always thought was as solid as a rock is not and the government that you think will come to your rescue and give you 100% compensation will not. And the law that you think is on your side is not there to protect you either!

This true story, will anger you, it will frighten you and it will move you to tears. More than that, *it will force you to take action to protect yourself and the ones that you love.*

Because when a top London bank collapsed their innocent customers were not protected or compensated. Instead the innocent were abandoned by their government who simply watched as the victims were viciously hounded into bankruptcy. As for the law in the UK, it not only allowed the innocent to be persecuted it fully supported the receiver to the bank that had gone bust and gave those receivers the legal right to completely destroy the bank's innocent customers!

It gave those receivers the legal right to attack the innocent victims' businesses, their homes, all their live savings, all their possessions, everything. The law in the UK today in 2012 remains unchanged.

As British law is the model adopted by many nations in the world billions of innocent people throughout the entire world are at great risk and danger right now. Here is the graphic true story *that reveals what you never thought would have been possible.* Here is the truth that the general public were not supposed to see!

Here is the truth of how the innocent were treated not in some lawless primitive country but in one of the most civilized countries in the world, in the United Kingdom.

Be prepared to be shocked to your core. When you have finished reading this book you will learn why the government stood idly by.

It was simply because to protect and to compensate the innocent would simply have cost too much money!

In fact it was a far cheaper option to abandon the innocent and to forget that they ever existed.

Here is the true story! Of one exceptional man and his family! Who were the victims of a London bank that went bust! From the man who built a £200 million pound property empire from scratch and who was 'given' just twenty-eight days to save it!

This is the extraordinary *real life story of his fight for survival. The story of* business warrior: Paul G Salter.

This book tells the incredible and extremely painful cruel true story of one self-made man's fight against a bank that crashed, its official receiver and the law in the UK.

Paul G Salter is one of life's true fighters! A business warrior! Having been born into poverty, in the rugged windswept Fens of north Cambridgeshire. Where men are not so much born as they are forged from hard steel.

He left home at seventeen and by twenty-four he had made a fortune in buying and selling property. At only thirty-two he had single-handedly built a property empire worth £200 million pounds. *Everything was perfect. Until one day one bank that he dealt with collapsed* and he was served with a formal demand to repay a loan in full, in cash in just twenty-eight days. The amount was one million pounds!

Failure to do that would mean the collapse of his own £200 million pound self-made property empire and the loss of his home, all his life savings and every possession too.

The only problem is that in a deep recession property has no value and with a government not being in the slightest bit interested in coming to your rescue, with the law standing very firmly against you and being completely on the side of the receiver to the bank that had just gone bust *you are very alone!*

In fact you have just become two things: first, *you are an innocent victim,* and second, you have just become *a forgotten statistic!*

Most people in life encounter failure and loss, in death or love, marriage, business, employment, friendship and the rest, we all cope differently.

Imagine being the innocent customer of a bank that has just gone bust on you, imagine being given just twenty-eight days or lose a £200 million pound fortune and imagine if you can losing your home, all your life savings and everything else that you possess too.

How would you feel? How would you cope?

This book reveals the whole truth of how one man stood alone and fought for survival.

The kill took just twenty-eight days and the carnage that followed lasted for years!

Paul G Salter

CONTENTS

PREFACE 23

MESSAGE FROM PAUL 25

CHAPTER 1 29
THE NEWS. MONDAY 8 AM.

CHAPTER 2 32
WHAT THE HELL DO I DO NEXT?

CHAPTER 3 37
YOU HAVE NO LEGAL RIGHTS! YOU HAVE NO DEFENCE!

CHAPTER 4 41
TUESDAY AT LINCOLN'S INN

CHAPTER 5 48
WEDNESDAY, 9 AM

CHAPTER 6 53
AUCTION OR HELP?

CHAPTER 7 63
THE WISE MAN

CHAPTER 8 67
THE CITY OF LONDON

CHAPTER 9 75
A VERY SCARY NEW WORLD

CHAPTER 10 80
THE HIGH COURT SHERIFF IN THE BUSHES!

CHAPTER 11 84
TAKE HIM DOWN

CHAPTER 12 100
THE JOURNEY TO GERALD

CHAPTER 13 104
NO JOKE

CHAPTER 14 114
SERIOUS HEALTH ISSUES

CHAPTER 15 119
DIRTY WORK

CHAPTER 16 122
LIVING ON THE BREADLINE

CHAPTER 17 129
THE BUSINESS TENANCY

CHAPTER 18 134
I ALMOST GAVE UP TRYING

CHAPTER 19   149
THE LONG ROAD TO RECOVERY

CHAPTER 20   154
THE FINAL HURDLE

CHAPTER 21   158
THE GAMBLE

CHAPTER 22   165
THE DEAL

CHAPTER 23   170
TRUE LOVE CONQUERS ALL

CHAPTER 24   164
*BEGINNING AGAIN – THE ADVENTURE CONTINUES
"FROM ZERO TO HERO!"*

CHAPTER 25   179
THE INNOCENT MUST BE PROTECTED

PREFACE

What does happen when a bank collapses and a government does absolutely nothing to rescue their innocent customers? Or what happens when a government can no longer afford to keep a bank afloat?

This shocking true story tells you what really did happen in the UK.

You will discover how their innocent customers were treated, you will learn what happened:

- To their businesses, to their employees and to their families too!
- What happened to their home!
- What happened to their life savings!
- What affect the bank's collapse had upon a wife and children!
- And what happened to their health!

This powerful and shocking book explains in intimate detail what really happens when innocent customers of banks that go bust are not given protection and compensation.

MESSAGE FROM PAUL

The cruelty so graphically detailed in this book must never be allowed to happen to anyone ever again, the innocent must be protected!

It is absolutely essential that every government in the world pass new laws now, to protect the billions of innocent public that they serve and represent. Governments must give the innocent 100% protection and 100% compensation against banks that go bust.

No human being on our planet should ever be made to suffer as I did!

Paul G Salter

The beliefs that kept Paul going

- Failure is never an option!
- Get up every day of your life to win!
- Be polite, humble, honest and true!
- Expect the worst and prepare for it!
- Concentrate and focus all your thoughts, then take action!
- Try. Three little letters that mean so much!
- Rise above every obstacle!
- Never give in, or lay down and die!
- Remember, every day is a wonderful gift, enjoy it!

CHAPTER 1
THE NEWS. MONDAY 8 AM.

It was 8 am January 8th 1990. A typically normal cold, wet Monday morning. I was shaving in the upstairs bathroom, when the letter box slammed shut, followed by a shout and knock from the postman.

Half awake and half-dressed I descended downstairs, to answer his call.

"Just one for you to sign, sir," was his cheeky cheerful smile, which I ignored, as my mind was aroused! Strange I thought, to sign for something usually meant serious trouble or a least a special delivery of some kind?

And there was certainly 'no' trouble that I knew of!

I signed, for what appeared to be a perfectly ordinary envelope and went into the kitchen to make the customary English breakfast pot of tea and collect a glass of ice-cold orange juice from the fridge, in readiness for my pregnant wife.

Boiling that morning's kettle, I recalled just how lucky I was! I had married, my second marriage, the girl of my dreams, my original teenage sweetheart, Mandy.

We were just nineteen and seventeen when we first got together but the relationship did not last, as is usual in most young love stories.

Ten years and two failed marriages, one for each of us and two fine sons for me, had passed and then by some miracle we met again and married.

Sadly, at first Mandy was told that she could not have children!

Yet once we started to date again she immediately fell for our beautiful twin sons, William and Alexander, who were now approaching two and a half years old.

I felt so lucky and happy!

I had beautiful sandy blonde-haired children with great big brown eyes and a radiant wife who I loved tremendously!

I had a very close knit family of my own, something which I never had as a child and I had built a booming £200 million pound property empire from scratch, without the help from anyone.

My home was full of lots of business friends and parties!

I owned a stunning 'picture postcard' thatched home set in five acres of tall Hawthorne-hedged paddocks, full of top ponies for the children and there were the customary Mercedes sports cars and Range Rovers that go with the package!

Not bad for a boy born into poverty in the wild windswept Fens of rural Cambridgeshire.

Yes, at just thirty-two, I had the lot! I had achieved the dream!

A dream that in the next five minutes was to become an absolute nightmare that, later and not jokingly I would call 'my day mare'.

Mandy was propped up, as comfortably in bed as she could, nestled between the pillows, waiting for her tea and juice and wanting a first kiss of the day and of course a chat about 'the day's plan of action'. We always had one!

I prepared the brew in the way I knew that she liked best and opened that fateful letter.

The colour drained from my face as it contorted in agony. My hands shook. My breath was lost. My head hurt painfully as though someone had hit me in the skull with a hammer!

As I read:

Dear sir,

We write to inform you that we are the administrators for Chancery Bank, of London. Your loan of £1 million pounds must be repaid in cash, in full, within the next 28 days. We remind you that both you and your wife have both given personal guarantees for this loan.

Yours faithfully,
Greene and Clarke Accountants, London.

Seeing that I was in a state of full shock, Mandy seized my hand and I remember her shouting, "Paul, talk to me what is wrong?" And repeating those words again and again for what seemed like an eternity.

After a pause that seemed like years, I coughed and held the pain in my heart. "Mandy, Chancery have just gone bust, we have borrowed £1 million pounds to buy those two town centre development sites in Holbeach and the receivers want their money back now! And we are both personally liable!"

Even though the letter said 'administration', which sometimes means that the collapsed bank might be taken over by another and then resume trading, my sixth sense told me different and I could not lie to the lady that I loved.

Thinking about that morning now and looking back it was a miracle that she did not miscarry our youngest son, Harrison.

In fact now twenty-two years on in 2012, I wonder if the shock caused on that fateful January morning actually shaped the character and destiny of the son who was about to be born only eight weeks later?

Because if there was ever a more determined and strong-willed fighter in life, it was him!

CHAPTER 2
WHAT THE HELL DO I DO NEXT?

Both Mandy and I were shell shocked! So deeply shaken to our feet, that neither of us could speak and to think hurt!

Bravely, I hesitantly ventured, "Look Mandy, things are not so bad, the receivers will be reasonable, they have to be. I know things are tough right now in the economy and that good old Maggie Thatcher's government has just pushed the bank base lending rate up to 17%, but we are very strong financially and if Chancery go completely we will sail around that problem."

But even as I said it as calmly, reassuringly and as professionally as I could, I knew we were in for big trouble.

"Look we own £200 million pounds worth of prime property, in excellent locations, in many town centres in East Anglia. We have got other great banks that we are dealing with and in all we only owe £7 million, so if the receivers will not help us, then our other lenders will." And added, "We must be the strongest property group in the country."

And with those best chosen words, she smiled. Just!

For once I felt afraid. And, I continued, "We only owe them a million quid and as security they have got those two brilliant town centre sites, that we have just got planning consents for. One site now has permission on it so that we can develop a supermarket. And the other now has consent for thirty-four flats. They can't just demand their cash back and ignore those assets can they?

"Surely what this letter should say, if anything is sell those properties! Then pay us your loan back and keep the profit that you make, or refinance the loans that you took out with another lender, and then pay us the amount back that you originally borrowed.

"I mean, that is the logical way to go about this isn't it?" I added, "Net we are worth £193 million! Nothing can go wrong can it?"

And she smiled a little more!

But as I spoke those final words, I hoped they were right but I knew something was wrong, very wrong! For there was something sinister about the way the letter was worded and it bothered me.

The words in full... in cash... in 28 days... and both you and your wife are personally liable.

Yes, I was gravely concerned and very seriously troubled. But for Mandy's sake, I tried as hard as I could to not show it! But as we were soul mates, I knew that she knew too.

So I left the comfort of the bedroom, the tea and juice and hurried downstairs again to telephone Garry, my brother-in-law and right-hand man.

"Garry, Chancery have gone bust! The receivers are appointed and the shit has hit the fan."

His reply was completely un-phased and as calm as ever as though he already knew my dreadful news.

"Paul, look we must be one of the strongest companies in the UK! We will go to see the receivers today and sort any problem out that they may have."

I had discovered a true friend and gem in Mandy's brother, for not only was he one of life's true gentlemen, he was loyal, very bright and dedicated to his business life, with me.

Those were his good points!

His bad points were that his office was a mess like someone had thrown a bomb into it, and he was always so cheerful, both of which at times really irritated me.

Anyway, go to London that very morning, we did!

The train journey from Huntingdon station to London's King's Cross was painfully slow. We had missed the fast and packed early morning commuter coaches and instead had boarded one of the vacant later trains that served every local village along its route.

There we were, two 'yuppies' young upward professional whiz kids, of Thatcher's, late '80s, boom years. Dressed in the finest Italian double-breasted pin striped suits; striped starched collar shirts, bright silk 'Tie Rack' ties and black brogue shoes.

As we rattled along past frozen fields and farm animals, I reflected on the many years in business that I had known and of the social history that I had learnt at university.

I recalled that the UK, since World War Two, had been doing very well, with the exception of a few periods of national strikes and conflicts, here and there.

In fact the late '80s in particular had been a time of great prosperity and boom and if anyone would have been less than positive about the economy then, you would have considered them to be mad.

But as in the song, Bob Dylan said, 'Times They Are A Changing'.

Immediately following the Christmas holiday of 1989 it was as though 'someone had turned the tap off'. The 'free flowing waters of prosperity' were shut off. Maggie had decided that her 'iron rule run economy' was expanding even too fast for her. So what did she do about it?

Why, she simply put the bank base rate up to a whopping 17% and crippled every business and mortgage holder in the country. And she did not care a fig, 'this lady is not for turning' was her famous saying and was ultimately to be her downfall too!

Still, there I was, stuck on a cold train with Garry and feeling very vulnerable. Never had I been in a situation like it before. I was being forced to enter a brand new alien territory and I felt naked!

On arrival in London that afternoon, we jumped into a cab at the rank and speed off around the grey city narrow and packed streets towards our destiny.

As the taxi screeched to a halt, I tipped the driver handsomely and ascended the steps of the plush Georgian bow-windowed building that I had trodden so many times before, only this time things were very different.

Inside at the reception there were new staff that we had never seen before.

Suited and booted, Garry and I introduced ourselves to an elderly lady who looked down her nose at us.

Shortly a small, thin bald man with light blue, almost transparent eyes appeared and stood in front of us in the reception lobby.

"Mr Salter," he announced to me. "I am the Official Receiver for the bank and I cannot negotiate with you. You have your letter that I have written to you and you must consult, not with me but with your solicitor. Representing as I do the bank, we have properly demanded that your loan be repaid and matters are as simple as that! So good day to you gentleman, I really do have important business to attend to!"

That was all he said, as he turned away from us and left us on our own. And that was that!

Frank, to the point, clinical and cold. Goodbye and above all else obviously final!

So we were efficiently and mechanically turned away. And we went.

Anxious, worried and dreading the task that lay ahead and in waiting!

CHAPTER 3
YOU HAVE NO LEGAL RIGHTS! YOU HAVE NO DEFENCE!

During the train journey home I used the newly invented mobile telephone! It was the size of a house brick, weighed as much and was just about as efficient! Much to the annoyance of the other strangers in our second-class compartment.

In fact during our frustrating journey, one elderly lady hurled a torrent of abuse at me and tried to hit me about the head with her handbag!

Apparently she objected to me 'cursing' every time I had a call disconnected, which frequently happened, when I was half way through a sentence.

I tried to explain, that it was not my fault that the technology was so bad and that when I finally did succeed and get a connection, that I had to shout in the telephone at my end to ask the person on the other end to shout back, so that we could hear each other talk!

But she was having none of my excuses!

Much to the rib-cracking laughter, coming from Garry, who was rolling around the threadbare train seat, in stitches of laughter!

Apart from that bodily assault from a seventy-year-old strongly built lady, I did manage to succeed in contacting two of our solicitors that our companies used, on the tracks back from London.

One solicitor that I used a lot, for buying and selling property was based, on our main line, to the north in Peterborough and another, a short drive north again at Wisbech. Thankfully, both could see Garry and I late that afternoon and evening.

And I did manage to contact Nick, one of my directors from our office, to meet us at Peterborough station, with our legal contract, which Mandy and I had signed with the collapsed bank, Chancery.

It was fair to say that Monday 8th of January 1990, was turning out to be very memorable.

But nothing could prepare me for the revelations that would come to light, in the next few hours.

When Garry and I stepped onto the platform at windy and wet Peterborough, Nick was already running towards us, clutching his brown leather attaché case under his right arm. His face was bright red from the running, which I thought was unusual for a karate black belt.

Or perhaps, more likely, it was the importance of the package that he was carrying and the urgency of it all, that made his face glow like a red hot poker!

"I got the original documents that you want off the Chancery file, Paul," he spurted. "Every bit of paperwork that you insisted that I get," he added dutifully and he proceeded to hand me the brown A4 envelope, from his well-worn financial director's case.

"Thank you, Nick," I countered. "Now drive us to Billings and Peterson at Park Road and then we must go to Stoddards at Wisbech too.

"And Nick, do call your wife and tell her we are all working late tonight. And here, you can use my mobile telephone to do it," I added devilishly.

At this point in time, on that fateful Monday, I still managed to retain some sense of humour but that was going to change!

Jan Limming, at Billings and Peterson was like my mum. She was middle-aged, calm, quiet and kind, which fooled most people, especially as she was exceptionally bright and streetwise. In fact she was very much like a modern-day *Miss Marple*.

This day she was totally focused and entirely engrossed in studying every word of every letter in the doomsday folder.

For sixty minutes Garry, Jan and I had sat in total silence. Then at precisely an hour after we had entered her ground floor office, Jan delivered her opinion.

She was normally a very jovial soul but she knew the gravity of the situation and this was no laughing matter.

Even Garry, who at times of great adversity, came out with stupid one-line jokes, was solemn and still.

We held our breaths as Jan took off her gold-rimmed reading glasses and spoke very softly and deliberately, "Boys, I am now going to telephone London. You must go to Lincoln's Inn tomorrow for a top barrister's opinion and I shall come on the train with you. Things are not straightforward, and I am sorry, they do not look too good either."

None of us said another word, for we all knew what she meant.

The second meeting with Tom Heart, at Stoddards at Wisbech, later that evening turned out to be a carbon copy of the meeting with Jan.

We sat in silence and in awe.

Tom was a blunt, straight-talking Fenman and I respected him for that.

So now we waited patiently, for our second legal opinion of the day. Only this time, the dry and to the point delivery from him, went into much more sinister detail.

"Well guys," he said, leaning back in his high deep-buttoned red leather chair and holding his folded arms behind his thinning white head, "you are up the creek without a paddle, in my opinion.

"You Paul and your good lady Mandy, have signed clauses that state very clearly to me, that given the circumstances that you now unfortunately find yourselves in, that the official receiver is perfectly within his rights to forget that he holds charges on the two sites that you have purchased with your Chancery loan in Holbeach and that he can demand that you pay him the amount you borrowed in cash, within twenty-eight days and the law of this wonderful country is on his side. And that is my belief.

"But," he added, "do go with Jan to London tomorrow, give her my kindest wishes and may God be with you all and please Lord, let some brainy barrister prove me wrong!"

Somehow every fibre in my wretched body knew he was right but, for Mandy's peace of mind that night, I tried very hard to pretend otherwise.

CHAPTER 4
TUESDAY AT LINCOLN'S INN

Garry and I both met Jan as agreed at 8.30 the following morning at Peterborough station, so that we could all catch the express commuter train and travel back to London together.

The weather, like our fortunes had worsened, and the cold bit into my shaking body.

After receiving the advice from both Jan and Tom, two professional solicitors that I really respected, I felt sick to the pit of my stomach!

I had not eaten the night before, I had no appetite for food. Even though Mandy had gone to the trouble of preparing one of my favourite dishes, of sirloin steak with homemade creamy pepper sauce and fries, which in itself was special, as I like chips. So I disappointed my dear wife, who did her utmost to reassure me that 'things would work out just fine'.

Instead I spent the evening pacing around the living room! To such an extent, that you could see my footprints in the carpet!

Garry had stopped for dinner, which he consumed like a wolf who had not eaten for a month. Then he spent the evening telling stupid jokes about the dilemma and that made me feel even worse.

As for the two bottles of red wine that I helped the others consume, they did nothing to relax me and I slept very little that freezing Monday night.

As the train rattled, speeding on its 50 minute journey, I half interestingly listened to the conversation of my colleagues. Slowly I drifted away into a world of my own.

I kept seeing the face of the official receiver. He was not angry. In fact he was extremely placid and totally devoid of any emotion. His face was expressionless. It was hard and uncaring and unkind.

I imagined that he must have had no love as a child and that fashioned him to become the granite like robot that he was. A humanoid just doing a task he had been programmed to do. I was certain that I would not find any pity or compassion with him at all!

I then thought about Mandy. With her in child, and I imagined how insecure she must be feeling.

I thought deeply too about our little twins and about my two elder sons from my first marriage who I loved dearly and who I missed every day tremendously. I began feeling emotions of uselessness and of loneliness that had not surfaced before!

I remembered my granddad who had just died, who I was very close to as a child. We had lived in the same tiny Fenland village of Gorefield and when my mum and dad argued as they often did, I would escape and visit my grandfather. Oh, I missed him so very much. Now even he had left me!

It was on that Tuesday fast train service that I fully reflected on the fragility of my situation, and of my love for those around me and of my concern for their well-being. My concern for myself was not important. I was frightened for them. How would they cope, if in the worst case everything went horribly wrong?

That was the biggest single thought in my mind, as we hauled into King's Cross Station!

I did not realise it at the time but I had entered a period of deep subconscious shock!

These emotions, feelings and images swirling around in my brain had started to consume me. I can now only liken it to being awake but being detached from reality. I was drowning in my own sorrow for my loved ones!

I was absorbed in morbidity and I started to get snappy!

As we were waiting in the rank for the next cab to take us away, Garry's silly happy mood, was really starting to piss me off when he innocently said, "We'll get this sorted today, mate, and then you and Mandy can jet off for a quick hol before the baby is due."

I went mad. I grabbed him by the collar of his trench coat and pulled his face to mine and told him straight, "Fucking shut up, or else!"

Jan dived in between us and pulled us apart! It took all of her strength to intervene.

After a few seconds I came to my senses. "Sorry Garry, this situation is very serious and the very last thing on my mind, at the moment, is flying off abroad on holiday," was all I could say!

As the perfect gentleman that he was, he apologised to me. Garry had just entered the really serious world that I was now firmly occupied in!

And we spent the rest of our short time together, from that day onwards in sobriety.

So through the streets of the city of London the three of us travelled in silence.

We arrived at the green oasis of the barrister's quarters, adjacent to the High Courts of the land. Number 7 Stone Buildings, Lincoln's Inn, with its giant black highly glossed sixteen-panel door was a place I knew and hated!

And Daniel W. H. Smythe, the brainy barrister that Jan had chosen for us, was a man that I disliked even more, even if he was on our side!

His public school 'plumb in the mouth' accent, welcome 'you jolly old boy' demeanour and the way his fees went up faster than a rocket could fly, grated on me big time.

And I was certainly in no mood to be messed with!

Daniel was a small, fat, cigar chain-smoking, weasel, with a piggy pink face and a turned-up nose to match. In fact if he had a little curly tail sticking down the back of his black and white striped trousers, I would not have been in the least surprised!

Yes, he was in his mid-thirties and was a physical wreck. And he used far too many foul four-letter words even for my liking. But, luckily for me, he possessed, probably the sharpest business brain in the UK, was as sharp as a cut-throat razor, and he knew it. And he got paid very handsomely, for it too!

So, I took some comfort for being in his fourth floor office.

Yes! If there was anyone who was going to save Mandy and I, then it was Daniel. Heaven help us!

As I expected, Daniel took twice as long, as Jan and Tom, to give me his answer. A full two hours precisely. As all barristers and solicitors charge by the hour, it is no surprise to me that they start and finish on the hour.

Then when he was ready to give us the full show of his dramatic presentation, he leant across his giant paper-bundled filled, leather-topped desk looked me straight in the eye and said, "Sorry old son, this time, you are fucked! The receiver to good old Chancery Bank has got you banged to rights. There is no defence. Not even I can get you off the hook.

"You see Paul, both you and Mandy innocently signed up to the small print here," at which point he stabbed the document with his right index finger. "This clause states very clearly that in the event of Chancery Bank having a receiver appointed to themselves, that the receiver can completely ignore any assets that the bank holds as security against any loans made by the bank and that the receiver can call for the bank loans to be repaid in full, in cash, in twenty-eighty days, and both of you signed to say that you agreed with that clause. Both you and Mandy have innocently signed cast iron guarantees.

"You have both signed your own death warrants. I feel sorry for you both, I really do, and God knows who would have ever expected good old Chancery to have crocked it? But there you are they have, so the official receiver has formally called for his pound of flesh and you must deliver it on time, or face a winding-up order for your companies and I have no doubt welcome bankruptcy petitions against both Mandy and yourself.

"And you have no time to fanny about and try and be clever either, it is time for you to piss or get off the pot, dear boy. However," he continued, all is not lost. You still have twenty-six days to beat the clock, and I know from our past dealings, Paul, that you are fast on your feet and very resourceful when you have to be. Do not waste one minute of the precious time that the receiver has given you. Go now, sell those sites in Holbeach or sell anything else that you can, or go and rob another bank if you have to, but whatever you do, go now! And do not even think about fighting the law over this one because there is not a judge in the land that will help you fight the documents you both signed.

"Come up with the cash and you both go free, if not, it is curtains for sure, for you and yours. I am very sorry, but it is as simple as that. The law in our Great Britain allows the receiver to get his one million pounds off you in cash in twenty-eight days. And until the law in this country is changed there is absolutely nothing that I nor anyone else can do to help you!"

And with that final word on the matter, he rose to his full five foot three inches, held out his podgy swollen hand, and said, "Goodbye."

I felt sick because the very brightest brain I knew in the UK had just told me that the receiver had Mandy and I over a barrel just because of the tiniest of small print in an obscure corner on the back page of an A4 piece of paper, said that if Chancery Bank went into administration that their receiver could demand the loan repaid, in full, in cash, in twenty-eight days, and that was that!

We had innocently signed our agreement to that tiny clause. But who the hell could ever have predicted that the London bank that you were dealing with would ever in a million years have gone bust?

But gone bust they had!

Now it was a fact of life and the receiver was, 'just doing his job'. Sadly Mandy and I were just innocent customers. Up to that point in time, we had an extremely successful business for we had not collapsed, we had done nothing wrong! We had simply taken out a loan with a London bank that had got itself in a financial mess of its own making!

Chancery Bank had gone down the swanee and we were a trapped innocent family.

Unfortunately for us, entirely unlike the Labour and Liberal Democrat/Conservative coalition governments of 2008, 2009, 2010 and 2011, the Thatcher government of that day refused to come to our rescue, and neither would anyone else!

We the innocent customers of the collapsed Chancery Bank of London, were left unaided, we were abandoned, we had to fend for ourselves.

The receiver had the law of the UK, firmly and cast ironly on his side.

We had time ticking by. We were on our own, and we were at the receiver's mercy! But he had none!

As we sat huddled together for warmth and not comfort in the back of the black hackney cab, I said to my two very grim companions, "OK, Daniel is absolutely correct, we have two options here. First, we must sell those sites in Holbeach, or anything else that we can, and secondly, we must go cap in hand to our other banks and ask them for their assistance and we must take immediate action in that sequence!"

Even before we had travelled to Lincoln's Inn that Tuesday, to meet Daniel, I had prepared myself mentally for the worst. Therefore I was shaken but I was not completely unprepared. In fact I was not shocked at what Daniel had told us that day. All Daniel had done was to make the picture absolutely crystal clear!

Yes, we were now about to be thrust into immediate action. Effectively this was war!

It was kill or be killed!

As I sat down with Mandy that Tuesday evening, beside a flickering open fire, I held her close and told her that I worshiped her, and sadly, I revealed my darkest thoughts to her, because I knew I would need her strength, to get me through the dark hours that lay ahead. And, to shield her from the truth would have been kind, but cruel, when reality had to be faced.

So I announced my battle plans to her. She was my closest, trusty and most faithful general. They say that, 'behind every great man, there is an equally great woman'. This was not to be in my case! No, behind me, just a mere man and a mortal human being was a supreme fantastic lady!

I could never have wanted for a more solid rock to turn to, in times of exceptional stress and danger. She was 'my everything' and through all the pain, she kept me sane! And throughout the history of the Chancery Bank affair and during the very many years since, I am eternally, in her debt.

Rising earlier than normal the following morning, on Wednesday the 10th January, I fully appreciated that in just forty-eight hours, that I had debated the crisis that I faced with the very best, and vitally importantly, most 'down to earth' business brains in the country.

I had got 'no holds barred' frankness. And I had the full support of my wife and my brother-in-law.

My mind was crystal clear. During my many years 'in the fast lane' of the business world, I had conditioned and concentrated my thinking process, to be laser sharp and seriously focused!

Now, I was prepared and ready to fight. I knew what I had to do, and I was hungry and eager to get into action. Now, I had to galvanise, my board of directors into a swift and lethal task force, too.

Arriving at our head office, I summoned all our key directors, for a board meeting. This I did every day at 9 am sharp!

For thirty minutes, the boardroom was locked, all calls diverted, no one not even Mandy disturbed our total concentration.

Every day started this way as we focused 'on the business in hand'. We listed from one to ten, our most important 'business projects' of the day.

I thoroughly enjoyed my work and I was proud of the directors that I had assembled around me. For each one was an expert in their own field: finance, construction, planning, sales and expert negotiators. I hand-picked the best.

We worked hard and played harder, and I rewarded them to the very best of my ability. Together, we were a formidable force, each director was a piston, in a highly efficient engine, and I was the driver!

On that Wednesday morning, instead of the usual ten exciting, 'money making schemes', there was only one item on the agenda.

Jayne, my completely trustworthy personal assistant, had prepared the agenda notes. She laid them out on the boardroom table, as myself, Garry, Nick, Jason, Mike, David and Andrew entered the room.

I had told her little, only that the words, 'Chancery Bank', were to be typed on a plain white piece of A4 paper and placed before each director's chair position.

"Good morning, gentlemen," I opened, as the grandfather clock behind my seat, chimed nine o'clock. "Before you is the agenda for today, tomorrow and the next twenty-five days! As from now, all other business will stop until the two words, 'Chancery Bank' are removed from this list!"

And so I went on, to explain in full detail, the events of the previous forty-eight hours, and the significance and the seriousness of it all.

They had all seen and heard the national television, radio and financial newspaper, headlines. And they all knew that, Chancery Bank, were one of the banks that we were currently doing business with.

"We are at war," I added, and every eye in the room was fixed upon me. "Chancery Bank receivers must be paid one million pounds, in cash, in full, in the next few days! That is what we must do. And," I said, "you, gentlemen have two options: option one, is that you can fight with me to make that happen, or option two: is that you can take your paid holiday and go and leave me alone to do it. Either way, I need your answer now!"

I had given each man a choice: stay and fight or cut and run. Each director spoke their turn.

And I was not surprised when 'all' vowed to stay and fight with me! And that is exactly, what we did.

"OK," I barked, "Nick, we do not have a minute to lose. Contact every property sale auction house in the country. I want everything that can be sold, put up for sale, and the rest of you work with and assist him. Thank you, and good luck, to you all, gentlemen!"

I was always polite to my fellow directors for, although we were a determined, driven, business force, to be reckoned with. We were all, respectful of each other's professionalism.

As they filed bravely, out of the boardroom that Wednesday morning, I added, "Concentrate fully and only on the task in hand, and maintain absolute silence outside of this room. Make no loose chat in pubs, clubs, wine bars, gyms or anywhere else. I do not want anyone outside of this boardroom, to get a whiff of this, and I mean absolutely no one! That means no secretary, no wife, no girlfriend, no one. Is that clear?"

All agreed that it was!

We all knew that idle talk causes panic and that panic is deathly dangerous. If this crisis, leaked out to 'the outside world', that we were wounded and in trouble, our creditability would be destroyed! Every current 'work-in-progress deal' could be lost. As rumours spread faster than any forest fire, and we were 'not' finished yet!

Before everyone left the boardroom that Wednesday morning I issued one final order.

"Oh, Garry, as you are the king of comedy, I want you to continue to tell silly jokes in this office and to keep everyone on their high normal spirits. Can you do that for me please?"

He duly agreed.

Garry was the last to leave the room that life changing Wednesday morning. As he turned to close the door and leave me alone, he bowed his head and said, "Paul, I am so sorry for you and Mandy." And then he left me.

Alone now, as he closed the door gently and softly behind him, I lifted the telephone receiver and said, "Jayne, get me the managers of all our banks, NatWest, TSB and Property Lending Trust, to start with, please. Also get me John Levy, Ken Singh, Peter Healey, Roger Portman and any other financier you can think of that we have had dealings with, past and present.

"Next please, I want Alan Knight and Rob Holden, our accountants, and last of all, can you get me a tea, strong, and black and in a mug but only half full please." And then I added, "Oh Jayne, thank you very much for everything, it really is most appreciated."

Now I was ready for war!

CHAPTER 6
AUCTION OR HELP?

Following that Wednesday 'war cabinet' meeting, everyone went silently and solemnly about their work. Despite Garry acting as 'a stand-up', as he normally did!

Very skilfully, I telephoned and asked our other banks, how they were finding things now that the interest rates had risen so dramatically, their answers were all the same. All new loans had virtually stopped dead!

Their use of the word 'virtually' only gave me a tiny amount of comfort!

Guardedly, I then spoke to every financier that I could to see what the state of the National Lending Market was and all confirmed my belief that since Maggie had 'hoiked up' the base rate to 17% all 'lending books' were closing fast.

The amount of 'new business loans' being done was paralysed. Maggie had succeeded in her aims and had stopped the expansion of Great Britain dead! Rigor mortis was advancing rapidly!

So my hope of refinancing the stricken loan with Chancery, 'realistically' with a fresh normal lender did 'not' exist!

And that advice came from the many financiers that I knew very well who 'in normal times' were only too willing to take my call then, run off into the financial market place and secure me an excellent loan often within minutes, because that was how they earned their fat fees!

Leaving 'no stone unturned' I then telephoned my clever accountants, to ask them the same question. "How is the, Property Lending Market? And do you know of anyone that is lending at the moment? Even in, the sub-prime market, that is, do you know of any lender, out there, anyone, anywhere, at all?"

Their answers were unanimous. "Sorry, Paul, no one we know of is lending anything. There are no fresh property loans being done, in the UK. Not even the loan sharks, are biting!"

The UK, they all confirmed had ground to a full stop!

Although I knew that every word they said was painfully true, I then telephoned every other person that I could think of. Even those with very 'unsavoury' reputations, all gave me the same answer. "The national situation is dire!"

No one anyone knew was lending to the property sector. They were actually trying to run away from it as fast as they could!

Because like the *Titanic* it was sinking fast!

In fact most of the drowning rats that had bought into the market when the prices of property were at their highest levels for a generation in 1988, were jumping off the ship as fast as they possibly could.

I was not surprised at what I learnt.

For Chancery Bank was not the only bank to have gone bust in the latter part of 1989. In fact they were the smallest!

For only a few weeks before them, another bank I almost had the pleasure of doing business with called British and Commonwealth Bank of London had gone bust! And then at the tail end of the year a massive outfit called The Bank of Commerce and Credit International had gone down with all hands. They had disappeared with hundreds of millions of pounds of local authorities' monies that had been invested in them.

In fact my best sources informed me that, they, BCCI Bank, had gone bust owing their creditors a whopping one billion pounds at least!

So basically, the Chancery Bank collapse was not unique and we were not alone. And now I knew where I stood!

I was under no illusions, we needed a miracle to survive!

Two weeks later, Garry and I were sitting on the back row of the seats in the ballroom of The Marriot Hotel in Manchester, the city where it always rains when I visit.

'King and Company' were the first of only two auction houses anywhere in the UK that we could all find to take our lots.

The collapse of the economy was driving an ice-cold and bitter wind through the industry, that January, for although the auction catalogue was full, the room was empty.

Apart from us two, there were only three other people in the room and one of them was the auctioneer.

He was a bag of nerves as lot after lot, nothing sold. And when I say nothing, I mean, absolutely nothing!

Halfway through his list, he paused for a leak and tea and I strode across the room to get his attention.

"Look," I said, "I will double your commission on lots, 304, 5, 6 and 7 if you can sell one. Also there is to be no 'reserve price' either. You are free to sell unrestricted and get any reasonable bid that you can! Watch for my nod at the back of the room as a signal, that I will take an offer. And please do tell the other two men in the audience that there is now no reserve on our lots."

And so, he did, as I offered. But as each lot came and went there were 'no' sales. That is correct, in fact not even one property sold that day!

On leaving the auction rooms it is quite normal to get a tap on the shoulder from a fellow person in the sale and to be asked 'if you would take a cheeky price', on an unsold lot. It's what we call in the industry 'getting a tap from a thief'. But that day there was no 'tap' and no criminals either!

The other two men in the sale room that day, like ourselves, must have been desperate sellers not in the least interested in buying, anything.

The Manchester sale was to set an identical pattern for the next auction at 'Teal and Taylor 'of London the very next day.

Similar to the Manchester sale there were very few people in the auction room and nothing was selling. Despite the auctioneer banging down his gavel pretending that he had just sold something to an imaginary buyer.

So no real sales and you guessed it, no 'cat burglars' either!

I tried desperately not to be downhearted, but the reality of the situation was overwhelming. The country was in the vice-like grips of the worst recession ever known to modern man. And the property industry, like the weather, was frozen solid.

On returning home from the Manchester and London sales, it was obvious that any buyers, with any money were not spending it!

Our educated guess at that time was that people were waiting for the property market to reach its bottom point before they made any new purchases, which I believed was a very wise decision on their part. However, that was not at all helpful for us, bearing in mind our perilous position.

Mandy remained, as always, supportive! And Garry did too. But both were looking for my leadership skills and thoughts as to what we must do next.

When we returned back to the office empty handed, the directors were naturally grief stricken and worried. For their own sakes and for that of their families and their own mortgages too. And although virtual silence was maintained in the office, dangerous little whispers had blossomed.

The girls in the office often hugged each other and burst into tears, and I found little to say, to comfort them, at all.

As the days ticked by the 'national recession' as it was now commonly called, was getting rapidly worse.

Suddenly everyone from the largest multi-national, to the window cleaner, were in serious trouble!

The national and local newspapers were full of the horror stories of the collapses of all sizes of businesses.

Regional companies, many of a hundred years and more standing, were going down by the dozen a day and still Maggie maintained her stance that interest rates should remain high.

Most business were paying 3% over base, so they were paying 20% interest and more!

Even the cartoonists, in *The Financial Times* and other respected national dailies and property trade magazines, were drawing pictures of people jumping out of skyscraper windows, with the captions: 'There goes another established businessman', or 'Poor chap, only, last week he was a very successful, property developer!'

And they were telling the absolute truth. It was no joke. People were actually committing suicide and jumping out of windows, and were finding other means of death as an escape from their miseries.

In fact, the godparent to William, one of my twins, a very senior and respected London financier, did try to kill himself!

One evening at home, I had a telephone call from his totally distraught wife, who sobbingly told me that he was in hospital and very near death following a deliberate overdose. Luckily he survived!

So now, the reality of the national, UK, economic crisis, had taken on a very personal tone. Ordinary innocent business people were actually killing themselves, as their businesses crashed. Many could not cope with the loss of their life's work, so they took their own lives!

Added to this, tens of millions of people in the UK were suffering because of the crippling high interest rates. For not only were businesses rapidly collapsing, also house repossessions were soaring too! For those who had lost their employment, or who could not afford the new crippling, high monthly mortgage costs that had been thrust upon them, they found themselves were, quite literally, being thrown out onto the streets!

For those who were lucky enough to stay employed, when their mortgage payments went 'through the roof' they had no income left to spend on anything else! Suddenly they were destitute too. Whichever way you looked at it, the country was in a chaotic bloody mess.

The reality of it all hit me like an express train. Thud! Like a punch straight to my nose!

Property now had no value! You literally could not even give it away. The auctions in Manchester and London had proved that beyond any doubt.

And 'cash was king'. But the problem was no one had any, and there was bugger all we could do about it. The only person alive in the UK, at that time who could have taken action and saved the misery of the masses remained resolute and did nothing.

Maggie came to no one's rescue. We were all abandoned and doomed!

So now, I faced what I knew was to be the biggest challenge of my life so far. I would need to ask my other 'good banks' for help. This was my last chance and it was my 'only' chance. And I was very petrified to ask for their help.

With my acute knowledge of the chronic state of the economy added with the advice and opinions, of the many professionals that I kept around me, I knew that my chances of success of getting help, even from a 'friendly bank' that I had done excellent business with for many years was about as good as being a 'snowball in hell!' Back against the wall, I had no other choice but to ask for their help and I hoped and, yes, I prayed, that because of my track record that I would be 'a special case'.

I prayed very hard, for my salvation! I telephoned the other banks that we were dealing with, and I booked appointments to see their most senior directors at each one's head office in London, the capital city of the country and the financial centre of the world.

Garry was to accompany me to those meetings and with me, he would fight a tremendous battle for survival. He would prove himself to be the very best man that I have ever seen under such great pressure.

I truly believe to this day that Garry came with me out of the respect that he had for me, and for the love of his sister, Mandy.

Together, we faced either success or complete failure. It was no longer as simple, as paying Chancery Bank's receiver off; it had become the fight to save the whole £200 million pound empire from certain death. Because if none of the other friendly banks came to our rescue we were finished. Sunk! History! Finished!

As Daniel had stressed, the receiver would act. His letter, deliberately written and sent, on Monday 8th January, by recorded delivery, was no idle threat. It was an ultimatum!

In the late days of January, we arranged those London head office, bank meetings with NatWest, TSB and Property Lending Trust.

But before we went to London, I told Mandy and Garry what our strategy would be. I had decided that come what may, we would make the best of the chronic situation. We would travel to each of our banks, with as much good humour that we could muster, and whatever the outcome, we would remain professional and polite, for we were about to meet long standing friends. Friends who were themselves in great trouble and in a time of danger and need.

We would respect their position and I knew from experience that they, in turn, would be respectful of us and of our position too. And it was with that frame of mind and attitude that we would go to London and meet our other lenders.

After all we had done nothing wrong! We were innocent customers of a collapsed bank and we were extremely successful and proven businessmen.

We were honest, honourable and proud of what we, our directors, our employees and our professional team, had achieved. And our 'good banks' and their managers had played a vital role in that success.

When we met them, we would thank them and tell them, that we were grateful for all their years of excellent service, and above all else, we were gentlemen, professional, and we were noble!

So began the battle for our businesses, our lives, our wives and children and the roofs over our heads, and for those that worked for us, and for their families and for their homes too!

Riches or poverty! This was it. Failure is never an option.

But just before we departed to London, something else, very important in the back of my mind was worrying me. Greatly, very greatly, indeed. It had been buzzing around in my head for days. And it was a very unusual thought.

I was actually worried about our success!

Let me explain. I had come to the conclusion that incredibly our success was actually our biggest weakness, and when I had grasped that concept, it made me realise just how truly vulnerable we were!

Because of our phenomenal success and due to my inventiveness and my shrewdness, I had built an empire worth £200 million pounds and achieved that with 'only' £7 million pounds worth of debt, which was an amazing achievement by any standards!

And this was giving me very grave and real concern!

It was then that I recalled the words of an extremely wise man, a legend from the property world that I both admired and respected.

Once when I had told him of my success story, he had patted me on the back and said, "Well done, Paul, but be warned, for I tell you this, if a man owes a bank ten thousand pounds then he is in trouble. But if a man owes a bank £100 million pounds, the bank is in trouble!"

That solid advice was now ringing like church bells on a Sunday morning in my ears. The fact that he had warned me of was this and he was, of course, correct.

I only owed £7 million, and that was spread between three main lenders and Chancery Bank.

Under these circumstances, I had become two things: First, being worth £200 million I was a great prize! Secondly, as I only owed £7 million pounds I was 'small time'. For if I had owed my banks £100 million, my wise friend was correct! I would have been a very important customer indeed! I would have been a big-time customer and one that they could simply not afford to lose! But unfortunately due to my high net worth, I was highly desirable for attack for anyone who wanted to get control of my business!

As a prize to my enemies, I was extremely big time! In fact I had unwittingly become the largest and juiciest piece of prime Aberdeen Angus fillet steak in Great Britain!

And the city was full of sharks who would greatly love to devour me.

Yes! It was now that I knew I was about to sail into extremely dangerous waters in the raging seas of the City of London, for in the confines of the financial square mile secrets are very hard to keep, and honesty and loyalty, especially where such vast riches are concerned, are rare! And I was mortified by all of those realisations!

As my wise mentor had predicted, I was indeed a small-time customer to my lenders, and I had become the richest 'takeover' prize in the United Kingdom!

CHAPTER 7

THE WISE MAN

Some people think, that to be successful in business, that you must be ruthless. I say that is very wrong. In fact, I totally believe that you need to be exactly the opposite: you need to be kind, humble and true.

For ruthlessness sits comfortably with greed, arrogance, selfishness, loneliness and unhappiness, and thankfully, in my life, I had none of those vices.

I never forgot the humbleness of my origins of my poor working class, small village childhood, of the kindness and warmth of my grandparents who had so little material belongings, but had so much love to give.

In particular, I was never greedy.

I often joked to my directors when we were on the point of selling a property that I had never been born a greedy man and that 'I was never going to start to be one now', especially when in the boardroom I was asked the question:

"Are we selling this too cheaply?"

My reply to that question was always this, "Look, we have made a decent profit and the people we are selling to must also make a profit too, for everyone in the chain has to eat. And if you push the prices up too much and squeeze the next guy in the chain and make him too uncomfortable, then he will not buy what we are selling, will he?"

With that profound simple logic combined with my complete lack of greediness, I had 'always' found buyers who were very keen to purchase from me and in fact, I did a great amount of repeat business with the very same purchasers.

Also this 'no-greed' policy had won me rave review with my banks who had seen me buying and selling my properties at an incredibly fast rate of knots. In their eyes, I was a shining star.

In my eyes, it was just plain common sense!

And so it was, we set off to see our three other bank friends at their head offices in London. It was then that I decided that our planned strategy had to be revised. Mindful of the sound advice of my very wise friend, I knew that I must not be greedy! In my forthcoming negotiations with my other lenders I had to be the opposite, I had to be extremely generous! If I stood any chance at all of surviving the crisis, I had to become a 'significant business' and one worth saving! Otherwise I stood the very great risk of being eaten alive by a predator!

Our new strategy had to be perfect, we would only get one chance of sitting before the senior directors of our three other banks as the twenty-eight days that the receiver to Chancery Bank had set were almost up!

There would be no second chances, the pressure was on me! I had to win! I had to clinch a deal with NatWest, TSB and Property Lending Trust and fast, or be stuffed. Better than a prize turkey on Christmas Day!

When Garry and I hit the financial streets of the City of London, I did not want them paved in gold and awash with my blood.

When we sat before the directors of our three, long-standing banks, I had to be the smartest and sharpest I had ever been in my life, or lose my life.

So, I sat down with my very heavily pregnant and lovely wife Mandy and with faithful second-in-command, Garry and, as always, I was brutally honest with them.

Basically I said this: "Look, the men that we are about to meet are first class people, they like us and we appreciate them, but they do not own their banks, they, simply run them as best they can for their shareholders.

"Also the directors we are about to meet, I would trust with my life. But not every person out there in the City of London is as pure. And we are severely wounded and are prey. So we must act swiftly and decisively, and this is what I want to do.

"I want your support on my proposal, please! If one, two or all three of our friendly banks help us and give us a new fresh loan to take over the two excellent town centre sites in Holbeach, and we pay off the Chancery receiver with his one million pounds in cash, we must reward them well! First very generously we will give them a 30% share in our profits from those completed developments or, if we chose to sell rather than to develop the two prime town centre sites in Holbeach, we will give them 30% of the profits on the sales income!

"Secondly, as an added incentive, I also wish to give those banks who come to our rescue, a 30% holding in our whole group of companies; for free!

"Yes, you heard me correctly! *For free!* So if all three banks come to our rescue that gives each bank a 10% stake in our total business for nothing! Or if only one bank helps us out of this mess they get all of the 30% stake!

"Basically, we reward them, for coming to our rescue in these unprecedented times. And that is my proposal.

"When normal trading conditions return, and when property regains its 'true value', my gift of 30% of our group will be worth the equivalent of £60 million pounds to those banks who came to our rescue!

"So with these exceptional offers, we have now become two extremely important things: first, we have become a very big customer to our remaining banks, and surely, therefore, we must have become a customer worth saving?

"And second, we have become immune from attack from an enemy, as we have joined forces with a very strong financial institution! I was convinced that my rare and extremely generous strategy was a winning formula!

After I had delivered my plan of action, both Mandy and Garry grasped the logic of my proposals, and to my delight, both readily agreed to support them. I was relieved and excited!

Now I could go into battle in the boardrooms of the City of London with some meaningful armoury.

I honestly believed that our other excellent banks would grasp my generosity.

And so Garry and I set off back once more to the square mile of the City of London.

CHAPTER 8
THE CITY OF LONDON

As Garry and I strode around the golden pavements in the City of London in late January, our spirits were high, even the constant drizzle and gathering dark clouds could not dampen our enthusiasm. Each of our other main banks had readily agreed to meet us just the same as they had always done. Normally when we attended these meetings, we were bursting with energy and we were very happy. Always we carried with us great news of yet another major business victory, we were the blue-eyed boys of the success of the late '80s. We were men who created and pulled off many multimillion-pound deals!

Before those fateful final meetings began, Garry and I knew that our mission was of a kind that we had never undertaken before. This time we were in the city not to announce our latest multimillion pound coup. This time completely unusually for us, we were there to ask for help.

However, with my soon-to-be announced uniquely generous package, I was quietly confident of success in securing with at least one bank, a rescue deal for our companies.

So Garry and I arose in the lifts of some of the tallest buildings in central London, and then waited patiently to be called into massive multi-panelled boardrooms. We sat positively before the directors of our three other long-standing and excellent banks at the head offices of NatWest, TSB and Property Lending Trust.

At the meetings at each bank, without exception, all our other lenders behaved as the absolute gentlemen that they were. As always, they were hospitable, polite and attentive. All were astounded and enthusiastic by my generosity. All were very kind and understanding.

And to a man, all were keen as individuals to do business with us. However, not one could help us. We were told with the deepest regret, that all property lending banks and other institutions in the city and throughout the length and breadth of the country, were under very strict orders that lending new monies to new property ventures anywhere in the UK was stopped with immediate effect!

Each bank told us, word for word, exactly the same story that they had been put under enormous pressure from both The Bank of England and their own board of directors, that lending on property schemes in the UK was finished until a day sometime in the future that they were told otherwise.

The Bank of England and their own boards had made it crystal clear that lending on new ventures must stop and stability must be restored to the property lending market in the United Kingdom, with immediate effect!

Lending more money to the property sector was forbidden and that exposure and risk could not be increased under any circumstances. And that was final! It was nothing personal.

If they had a choice they would assist us, but it was not negotiable because of the fear and absolute panic in the city caused by the collapse of three main London banks, of BCCI, British and Commonwealth and Chancery Bank just a few weeks earlier. This fact combined with the unyielding stance of the high interest rate policies of the Thatcher government, and the refusal of the government to go to the rescue of the fallen banks and their innocent customers, meant that lending more money to the UK property sector was now banned.

The effect of these factors had caused the City of London Property Lending Financial Market to be shut down. There was to be no more lending on any property ventures in the UK.

Consequently there was to be no rescue!

I swear, I even saw tears in their eyes as each director said the same, "We are very sorry boys, but from the top has come the very strict orders, no more property lending. And we fully understand that you had dealings with other banks and that the collapsed, Chancery Bank of London was one of them. But we cannot take over their one million pound loan for you; we cannot lend one more penny on any new property venture in the UK. The loan books, as far as property is concerned in Great Britain, are closed. They are firmly shut! And we cannot therefore make you a special case."

I was devastated. My world had just collapsed. I felt sick, hardly able to breathe. My throat felt that it had just been cut. I had nowhere left to turn to, I had exhausted all my options.

Although the boardrooms of each bank were filled with people, I was in a trance, lost to oblivion, cocooned in a world of my own.

The voices in each room seemed to slur. My vision did blur. My brain banged on inside my skull and my ears rang to the tune of giant brass kettledrums. Time ceased to exist!

It was only when Garry shook my left arm vigorously did I come partially awake.

I longed for those meetings in the financial City of London to be a bad dream, one that I wished I could awake from. But it was no dream, it was stark reality. It was a real life nightmare that I was totally caught up in.

Everything around me was like an out-of-body experience that was unfolding before me completely and entirely outside and beyond my control.

Like awaking from some hospital operation drug-induced sleep, I slowly and sluggishly recovered some composure, and coughed and blinked.

I tried as best that I could to negotiate my way out of the condemned cell in which I was trapped.

To every face that was looking at me around the room, I started to increase the amount of shares in my property empire that I was prepared to give away as a free gift. I even increased my offer to give away for free 50% of my business to anyone that would help me!

But my proposals met with a solid stone wall. It was just impossible for them to increase their exposure in a free-falling property market where the values of all properties: residential, retail and commercial alike, were plummeting by the day.

It was then that a thunderbolt hit me, property suddenly had no value. I could not even give it away!

The senior directors of our three other excellent banks listened to me very sympathetically but they could not, and they would not, come to my rescue.

They simply could not put another penny of their shareholders' monies into the British property market; they could not even put one more farthing at risk.

To be honest, in those exceptionally dark and desperate days of late January 1990, the truth was that no one knew how much worse the recession would get and no one knew just how long it would last for either!

There was one thing, however, that was absolutely crystal clear to the directors of those London banks and to us the professionals in the property industry, that for as long as Margaret Thatcher maintained her stubborn stance, with her high interest rate policy, that we and the whole country, were doomed!

With Maggie's iron grip on the economy and her blatant refusal to budge an inch, there was no end to the recession in sight.

Little did we know then that the Thatcher-imposed 17% and more high interest rate recession from early 1990 would cast its veil of death on the UK for years and years to come.

That recession was the most bloody in post-World War Two history and perhaps it could be argued that it was the worst ever known to man, where business and ordinary people by their millions would be sacrificed!

And so it was that the gentlemen directors of my other banks, for the sake of their shareholders, and for their own salvation, could not even take my very kind offer of a half share in my business. Even though it was a free gift worth £100 million pounds just a few weeks earlier. They simply did not intend to join BCCI, British and Commonwealth and Chancery Bank in the receivership club and in the dole queue. As hard as it was for me, I fully understood and I appreciated their position.

Even though it was a bastard for me to accept, on reflection, for what it was worth I did not blame them. Privately I would have come to the same decision had I been in their shoes. They simply had to save themselves and their own shareholders too.

And so with no government to come to our rescue and no one willing to take over the Chancery loan and being unable to sell any assets within the twenty-eight days allowed, we were finished. It was over!

All I had worked for and saved for all my life, due to the collapse of Chancery Bank, was lost.

Thatcher's government took no pity on us, in fact they abandoned us and the law in good old Great Britain was firmly on the side of Chancery's receiver. I could not get any more time than the twenty-eight days allowed under the law of the UK to save my group of companies.

And so that was that! I could not give the receiver of the collapsed bank what he demanded. He would he not get his one million pounds in cash, he would be denied his pound of flesh and he would go hungry!

Being completely alone and defeated, I then set into action the last plan that I had prepared with Mandy and Garry.

I looked each bank director straight in the eyes, gave them a firm but friendly handshake and thanked them personally for all their years of excellent business and I made a solemn vow too, that, one day, no matter how many years it took me that I would be back. Then we all parted company on as happy and positive note as my endurance would permit.

In four short weeks I had gone from being perhaps the most successful self-made young businessman in the UK ever in history, to being technically insolvent! We had gone from having a thriving business to having nothing, just because one bank that we dealt with had gone bust.

Our only crime was that we were just 'innocent customers' and we were victims of a loop-hole in the law in the UK that allows a receiver to ignore completely the sale of the assets that they holds as security and instead, permits them to call for their loan to be repaid in cash, in full, within only twenty-eight days!

Under these circumstances I could not continue to trade and I did not have any time left. I wanted to fight on, but my time had gone.

I knew, in my heart, that I would achieve success again and eventually of course I did within a few years. I did start all over again with absolutely nothing and I did return to enormous self-made riches again.

But at that moment in history in late January of 1990, I was dead in the water. Now I was faced with performing the worst task of my life so far.

And to this very day, some twenty-two years later, I still have nightmares on a very regular basis about it.

On my return to my office, I had to summon all my staff and tell them they were now unemployed. When I faced my loyal staff, most of the men and women were crying. I thanked them all from the bottom of my heart and it was broken. And in fact I had to tell them, that I could not pay any more wages. Not one more penny!

I explained to my staff, who I truly and sincerely called friends, that no blame was to be apportioned to our loyal previous lenders or indeed to the receiver of the fallen bank, they were after all 'just doing their jobs' and protecting their own positions!

The country had been plunged helplessly into a severe economic depression by the Thatcher government that did not care for us, the innocent customers of the collapsed Chancery Bank of London. There was no one to care for us or rescue us!

I had challenged the law, but it was very firmly on the side of Chancery's receiver, and we and all our families were finished.

I was exhausted, I could not have done any more. And all my staff and I knew that to be true. We were all powerless, the Thatcher government had imposed upon us all their high interest rate policy and we, the innocent, had paid the ultimate price and we were to be attacked and left for dead, and conveniently abandoned and forgotten.

And Mandy was about four weeks away from giving birth.

Now I was a lamb thrown to the wolves, my throat was exposed and the dagger was drawn across it, and it cut me faster than an eye could blink.

On day twenty-nine I received at 8 am another loud knock on my front door from the same cheeky postman.

"Another recorded letter for you to sign for, Mr Salter, if you will."

I had no choice, I signed for my own death warrant. I took it upstairs to my darling wife, and I read it aloud to her:

We, the official receiver for Chancery Bank, have formally demanded that you repay us your loan of one million pounds and you have failed to do so.

Consequently under the terms of the personal guarantees that you and your wife have both signed, we have instructed our solicitors, Berkings of Slough, to immediately apply for and obtain a winding-up order against the companies to whom Chancery Bank lent their monies and they will simultaneously petition for your joint bankruptcy.

The kill had taken just twenty-eight days and the carnage that followed was now about to begin!

CHAPTER 9
A VERY SCARY NEW WORLD

It was a miracle that Mandy did not go into labour there and then. It was also a wonder that I did not collapse with a heart attack, we had lost everything: our home, our cars, all our savings, my whole life's work, our dreams, everything!

I felt helpless, totally inadequate, very vulnerable and terribly alone!

I had done everything I could to prevent what had happened to us all! I had worked tirelessly and I had punished my body and brain painfully. I had not eaten or slept properly since the first letter arrived on Monday 8th January, the day that I will not forget for as long as I live!

Since that fateful day, I had been forced to make redundant all our wonderful staff, and that in itself, had taken a terrible toll upon my mental health as my mind was deeply tortured by their loss!

Now in addition to all of that, I knew that the whole affair would be reported in every local and regional newspaper, on all the local radio stations and on the East Anglian television channels too!

I was now also faced with the very public humiliation of our family and I truly believed that I was about to be branded a failure and be paraded publicly and cruelly before the local community!

I felt so ill at the prospect of being called a failure, a fool, an incompetent idiot, a loser and the rest. The thought of meeting neighbours or local village friends in a supermarket terrified me.

The image of me sitting with local people that I knew in my doctor's surgery, made me vomit! Just opening the front door of my home and stepping outside in the fresh air, disgusted me.

I felt dirty I felt thoroughly ashamed as though I was guilty of some terrible crime.

When the local newspapers did telephone me for my side of the story, I gave them an accurate picture. I told them that we were the innocent customers of a bank that had collapsed and that Chancery Bank of London had crashed of their own accord and that their downfall was their own fault. And I told them that the receiver to that bank had given me just twenty-eight days to come up with one million pounds in hard cash or be put into immediate receivership.

I also told them that I had taken a top barrister's opinion and that I had wanted to challenge the law, against the action that the receiver thrust upon me on the 8th January 1990.

I told them that I was informed by my barrister, who I rated as the very best in the country, that I had no legal defence to the hostile action of the receiver to the bank that had gone down!

In fact I told them that it was made brutally plain to me, that the law in the UK actually *allowed* the receiver to take the action upon me that they had done! I told the newspaper editors and the radio and television journalists too, the absolute truth. How I had attempted to sell everything that I could, but that as hard as I had tried that I could find no buyers in the precious little time that the law permitted me! Also that I had sought the help of our other financial organisations too, but that *no one* would come to my rescue!

And then I also said something which none of the journalists that interviewed me anticipated.

I took the opportunity of their interviews to publicly thank all my previous staff for their many years of support and loyal service to me and I told them how very proud I was of them all.

I also told the reporters that if I could help any of my staff and their families in any way that I could that I would do so. I made it crystal clear that our Fenland staff who had helped me build my business over the many years, those who worked for me in my office and the three thousand and more men that worked for me on our building sites and in the factories and warehouses on my industrial estates, that all of my staff were the true success of my businesses.

And that my staff were my greatest assets! That their families from Cambridgeshire, Norfolk and Lincolnshire were the very best employees in the country and that my heart was broken for them and for their wives and for their children too!

Later when I read the reports in the local and regional press and I heard the radio stations broadcasts and I saw myself on television looking a very tired and badly beaten-up figure, I sighed with small relief that every one of the reporters had presented a balanced report.

For I had sought no sympathy from them, for myself, what I had hoped and in fact prayed for, was for the sympathy for my staff and for their families because 3000 of them were now redundant, they now had no jobs, they had no money and they had precious little prospects either.

For not only had the Thatcher government of the time had abandoned me, worse by far, they had abandoned all of my staff and they had thrown 3000 excellent men and women onto the dole and the scrap heap of society.

Many of the men and women who worked for me did have a family, so realistically up to 10,000 poor souls were thrown into financial chaos and those good people of my beloved East Anglia, were suddenly very badly hurt indeed!

My soul was tortured and was bleeding for them out of sheer kindness, sadness, shock and grave concern.

The region's editors all wrote their scripts of 'the massive scale of the loss and of the real great human misery' that had fallen upon my companies and all of my employees simply because we were the innocent victims of a London bank that went bust!

And all of the media reports without exception were very kind and sensitive.

As the days turned into weeks, the burden of the tragic loss and human misery and suffering and of the failure on my part to save all the families who had relied on me for their employment preyed very heavily on my mind.

I could not eat and I did not sleep and as a result of which my health rapidly deteriorated. I weighed eleven and a half stones before the bank's crash, now I had lost three and a half stones and I quickly became a very frail eight stone skeleton.

Also my hair was falling out in handfuls, my teeth and gums would bleed and my face looked twenty years older. My eyes were sunken into the new deep sockets in a face that was so terribly thin.

Prior to the collapse of Chancery and to the crisis that now raged around me, I had been a young, fit, non-smoker, now I was more of a physical wreck than my barrister and the world around me was spinning so fast that it was difficult to keep in touch with any sense of reality.

In a very few days in the early weeks of 1990, I had gone from having everything that a man could wish for to having nothing. All my wealth, my director friends, my wonderful staff and my dreams were all gone.

All our so-called business friends that used to invite themselves to the garden parties at our home and who earned vast fortunes for themselves, by having their trades and surveying companies win contracts for work from my own group of companies disappeared straight away.

Many of which I never saw ever again.

Our cars were seized in our driveway by the receiver's bailiffs. And as all of my savings were invested in my businesses, I had virtually no money to feed my family.

I was so naive, I did not know what Income Support was. For months I claimed no benefits. Instead, we survived off the few hundred pounds that I had in cash and I returned to the poverty of my birth.

I felt, unclean and filthy, yet none of the sad affair had been my fault, yet despite it all, my spirit was not broken completely.

I vowed to Mandy, with whom I was now alone, that I would never lay down and die. And that some way, at some time, I would rise above the situation and I totally believed that to be true.

Yes, I had lost all my worldly goods, but I still had the love of Mandy and she showed me tremendous, care, kindness and affection.

Then eight weeks after receiving the first letter, demanding their one million pounds in cash, on the 7th of March 1990, our youngest son, Harrison, was born.

Suddenly I was a very proud man again and his birth and the joy of it was to be a major turning point in my life.

CHAPTER 10
THE HIGH COURT SHERIFF IN THE BUSHES!

With Harrison's birth came a new ray of sunshine. It was a turning point for me in a variety of ways.

Firstly, because I had witnessed a new bundle of love and joy being delivered into the world: a very cruel world indeed. Secondly and much more seriously, it was also a very great relief as I was gravely worried for Mandy and Harrison's safety.

But here he was, this miracle of life, this gift from God and with him came the hope of a better future that a child brings with it into the world born innocent and pure, his arrival said to me, 'look here I am, I am a new beginning. Let me prove to you what I can do'.

Positive thoughts flooded through my very seriously troubled mind. It may sound strange, but I could see how Harrison and myself were actually in a very similar position in life.

I knew that the receiver and their solicitors would strip me bare; they would sell all my assets and leave me naked. But like a newborn child, I, too, had hope for a better future and no man could take that hope away from me. They could take the shirt off my back, they could take every penny out of my pocket too, but they could never take my hope away, that was impossible, no matter what cruelty they inflicted upon me.

I kept telling myself that I would survive and much more than that, I would get back on my feet and become a success in business again and I would restore my family's wealth and reputation for excellence. Very slowly, at first, over many months I began to regain my self-esteem.

Do not get me wrong the path to mental recovery and to financial recovery too, was a very long and arduous road indeed. In fact, each and every day was in its own way was a battle for survival. To put it bluntly, I had been forced, beyond my control, to accept my new situation.

Naturally it took me some time to get used to my new life, but still there it was, I had no choice in the matter, fate had dealt me a seriously bad hand and that was that.

So I vowed to Mandy that I would get up every day of my life to win and as painful and hard as it was, I did.

It was then out of all this sadness that another event, took place, one which probably would have plunged most men into even more despair. Only to me it did exactly the opposite!

Like Harrison's wonderful and safe arrival, this next memorable experience was to make me happy.

One night in pitch blackness when I had returned home, from meeting my own newly-appointed official receiver, to my former group of companies, a man was lying in wait, hiding in the bushes of my driveway.

On seeing me walk past him, he jumped out and nearly frightened me to death.

"I am the County High Court Sheriff," he said. "And I have come to repossess all your furniture. I am coming into your home, I am taking your sofa, television and anything else that I want and I am coming in now!"

I am sorry but I thought the hiding in the bushes in the dark was so silly and childish that I just burst out laughing.

I said, "Are you really that desperate that you want to do that?"

"Yes," he said, and he repeated, "I am coming in now with this court order." And he waved a piece of paper under my nose.

I said, "Look, you have just repossessed all my business assets, they used to be worth £200 million pounds and it is 8 pm at night. I have three little children and my wife in the house, I am worn out and exhausted and to strip my home bare at this time in the evening, will cause them great distress. Can you please come back in the morning?"

To my astonishment and relief, he agreed.

At 7 am the next day he was banging hard on my front door. And this time it was my turn to give him a piece of paper of my own.

It simply read, in effect, as follows:

To whom it may concern, please note that all furniture and electrical goods, at my address, have already been sold, to a genuine third party.

He was too late, everything in my home was owned by someone else.

I could have found that note the night before, but I was so tired and exhausted that I did not want a confrontation with the Sheriff that evening, so I decided to let him wait until the morning before delivering my devastating news to him, as I guessed that he would be really angry, and my assumption was correct, he was very pissed off!

But there it was, it was a fact of life, in desperation and a genuine fear of starvation, I had sold everything, all the contents of our house a few weeks earlier because it was the only way that I could feed my family.

Now all my furniture and electrical goods were rented, everything was owned by another genuine third party and legally he could not take their possessions.

A very red-faced High Court Sheriff left hurriedly and empty handed.

You could virtually see the steam coming out of the collar that closed around his bright scarlet neck. Our furniture, television and our toaster were all safe and I never saw him again.

My innocent sale out of absolute need to put food on the table had turned out to be a stroke of good luck. Otherwise he would have taken everything and he would have left us with a bare home. Had he succeeded in taking our kitchen table we would have had no food and nothing to eat it on either!

That sorry and tragic incident actually made me feel as though I had won a little victory and my spirits were lifted ever so slightly. However, my tiny piece of happiness was about to be very short-lived.

I would soon need HGV loads of good luck as things were about to get a whole lot worse. In fact, matters were going to get nasty, very nasty, indeed!

CHAPTER 11
TAKE HIM DOWN

For the next two years the recession got worse and worse. The hope of a quick economic recovery evaporated, it never happened. The country was stagnant and dying.

I was now 'signing on' every other Tuesday morning at the Job Centre in return for which our family received the princely sum of £55 per fortnight. £27.50 per week to be precise on which to live.

There was no employment, no jobs of any kind, nothing!

To stop the boredom and in desperation I turned to doing odd jobs for neighbours, in my local village.

I would very humbly knock on doors and ask for work. I cut peoples lawns, washed their cars, chopped kindling. I did anything!

And I told the Job Centre what I was doing, so that I was honest and true at all times because I may have returned to the poverty of my birth, but I never was a criminal. I was an honest man and I lived my life by an honest code of conduct.

Meanwhile Berkings of Slough continued to write to me regularly.

Eventually some two years and a few days after the collapse of Chancery Bank, I was ordered to appear at court.

Up until that moment in my life I had never been inside a courtroom ever before, sure I had met Daniel, my barrister, on several occasions for top legal advice, but in fact I always avoided actual litigation whenever I could.

During my very many years in the fast lane of the business world, I had never crossed or ripped off anyone. I lived my life by what must seem to today's children to be very old-fashioned. I had been bought up as a child to respect my elders. I had been taught manners to always say 'please' and 'thank you' and I had been taught that to steal or to act in any dishonest way was a serious mortal crime, so for me to be summonsed into a court was a very new experience indeed.

On a day of torrential rain, numbers 204 and 205, of 1992, were ordered to the Peterborough County Court.

It was Tuesday 22 February 1992. A day I shall remember all my life.

Mandy should have come with me, but I saved her the journey and the pain. Instead I had decided that I would suffer the wrath of the judge because she did not go as demanded.

When I was called from the designated waiting area and led into the courtroom, I was told by the black draped clerk to the court to stand between two big beefy bailiffs inside an Elmwood compartment.

This new experience was daunting! Yes I must admit that I was nervous! But I knew that I was a completely innocent man! I breathed in and out very slowly and kept as calm as I could. It was true that through no fault of my own that I was forced completely beyond my control to make an appearance that Tuesday afternoon in the Peterborough County Court.

Just because I had been an innocent customer of a bank that had gone bust, that was my only crime in my entire life!

I was very poor, I was very beaten up mentally and physically, but I still had hope and I still had belief that one day in the future that I would rise above the punishment that I was now about to face.

So I stood and waited to receive my punishment. I knew that in the next few minutes that my beautiful wife and I were now about to be made officially bankrupt.

The clerk to the court voiced very loudly the next command in the proceedings of the day. "All rise!" he bellowed, "for his Honour Judge Coleman."

Every person in the second floor courtroom that day that faced onto the wonderful and gracious Norman-built Cathedral of Peterborough city centre, stood up straight away.

The middle-aged Judge Coleman looked at me in disgust from the very moment he entered the courtroom. Pacing towards the red leather high-back chair that stood the tallest of many behind a massive bench that was the highest point in the room, his face was grotesquely contorted and seriously angry!

There was complete silence in the room, no one dared to speak and no one dared to move. Everyone had their eyes fixed upon the judge, and he in turn, had his gaze very firmly fixed on me.

He lifted the corners of his raven-black cloak and fell into his lair – the tallest chair.

In fact I observed that his face and stoop gave him the look and posture of a raven with a thin face. With his long hooked nose and hunched-up shoulders, he appeared as if he was about to devour a rabbit that had just been killed on the road. When he leaned forward and studied me, he had the look of death on his face. He tilted his head to one side so as to look me up and down some more, his nose wrinkled and he sniffed. Then he sniffed again before recoiling in disgust as though he had just trodden in some dog poo.

For another minute he said nothing, he only stared. At long last this creature of the law spoke in a high-pitched and feminine voice, he crackled, "You sir, and your wife, are both charged with the act of bankruptcy. What have you got to say for yourself?" he boomed.

And at that moment he rose to his feet and pointed a stick like index finger at me. "Well?" he asked me again. "What have you got to say for yourself, man?"

I was not surprised by his strange, rude, childish conduct, in fact I had expected as much from him the moment he had dragged his reptile-like carcass into the courtroom. My guess was that he had a very bright academic brain and quite probably a public school boy education. I imagined that he was a cast-off boarder, a child that was abandoned at some well-to-do establishment and never allowed to go home!

My mind raced ahead and conjured him to be perhaps the product of some illicit affair so that when he was born he was condemned to be an outcast. Without the love of a real family, dumped as a baby at the gates of Tom Brown's School, whereupon he was left to rot.

Rightly or wrongly, I judged him to be a very clever man who took enjoyment showing off his well-developed brain and that he relished in being cold and to be cruel, too!

And I thoroughly believed that although he had offered me the chance to speak, that he believed that I would be too frightened to do so, well if he thought that, then I am very sorry, he could not have been more wrong!

I stood very straight and coughed to clear my throat, I got ready to give him my reply to his question and I was, as always, polite and honest. In fact I felt proud of my words that were recorded by the clerk of the court who typed them into a machine at the desk way below where the bird-like beak was sat.

I spoke out, clearly and loudly and I knew before I delivered my speech, that he was going to absolutely hate every word I was about to say but I did not give a fig what he thought of me and Mandy!

There you are, if he thought that by asking me *what have I got to say for myself* that I was going to feel ashamed or even embarrassed then he was wrong. What is more, if Judge Coleman thought for one minute that I was going down in the history book of the world as some timid little mouse of Margaret Thatcher's ruined economy, a forgotten statistic of her government then he was very wrong on that score, too! And so my much rehearsed and pre-planned attack began and it was Judge Coleman who was about to be taken by complete surprise!

So I began. "Your Honour, I am here before you today an innocent man. I was pursued into bankruptcy by the official receiver, of Chancery Bank of London, a bank who collapsed in January 1990 and I state for the Court Record that the law in this country must be changed immediately!

"I state that innocent customers like my wife and I, must be protected from attack by the receivers to banks that go bust, by our government and, more than that, that the innocent customers of banks that go bust, must be given 100% compensation for any financial loss that they suffer as a result of that bank's collapse.

"The British Government must be forced by law to 100% protect and to 100% compensate the innocent when banks go bust!" I then paused, and added, "When a bank collapses in this country it is wrong that their innocent customers should lose their businesses, their homes and all their life savings! And it is very wrong that they are hounded into bankruptcy. The law in Great Britain must be changed now!

I continued, "It is wrong to live in a country where the law allows the innocent to be driven into this: a bankruptcy court.

"In my particular case, the law and the government in this country has not protected or compensated me. It has abandoned me and my wife and our three little children.

"The law has failed and condemned me and the law of the United Kingdom has allowed the receiver to a bank that went bust, to destroy my innocent family! More than that, the law of this country has failed many other poor souls, too, who are not here today. For I employed many thousands of innocent men women and children that relied on me for their livings.

"Before Chancery Bank of London collapsed, I had an excellent group of companies with over 3,000 staff and most of them had families. In fact, in my case alone as many as 10,000 men, women and children have been forced to suffer tremendous misery because of the collapse of Chancery Bank! And I say that the antiquated and out-of-date laws in this country that state that we, the innocent, have no protection or legal rights to defend ourselves against a bank that has gone bust in the United Kingdom, is wrong! Very wrong indeed!

"So in answer to your question, Your Honour, I say that the law in Great Britain and everywhere else in the civilised world, in fact every country on this planet that has the same ridiculous laws, that those laws must be changed with immediate effect!

"The innocent customers of banks that go bust must be 100% protected and be given 100% financial compensation by their governments! Not only that, I say this, that every government, not only in the UK, but throughout the world, must be forced by tough new laws to take immediate action to protect the innocent, their families and their employees and their families too when a bank goes bust!

"And that all the governments of the world must be made by law to protect their innocent people. No matter whether a government is Conservative, Labour or any other political party or regime, they must be compelled to take immediate action to protect the innocent.

"And I also say this for the record of this court that new laws should make it *illegal* for governments to abandon the innocent customers of banks that go bust!

"In fact, if governments continue to not rescue and 100% compensate the innocent I say it is they, the government, that has been criminally negligent, and that it is they that should be sued for their non-performance!

"That is what I say, sir, for the records of this court today, Tuesday the 22nd of February 1992."

And I added, "I will not go to my grave until I tell the general public of the United Kingdom of my innocent persecution here today! Because this gross miscarriage of justice must be told to every man, woman and child in this country!

"The persecution of myself, my wife and my children must never be repeated in this country again! The law of the United Kingdom must be changed now. And I will campaign for that to happen until the day that I die!"

I then paused to catch my breath for about two or three seconds and pointing my index finger on my right hand to the judge, I said, "As for you, sir, that it is your job and duty to see that the law in the United Kingdom is changed forthwith and that you should put your efforts into getting the law changed!

"In fact I very strongly demand that you should join forces with me and make sure that the innocent people of this country are protected by the law. After all, protecting the innocent citizens of this country is what you get paid to do, is it not?"

And with that, without his permission, I sat down! That was word for word what I said.

And although he knew that every word that I had just spoken was true, Judge Coleman was not a very happy man!

Personally, I was very pleased with my speech. OK! I knew that I had repeated myself a few times but I had certainly made my point! I was defiant and proud and unbeaten, and he knew it!

I was on a personal crusade to change the grossly wrong and very bad laws of the United Kingdom, and he knew that too, and he knew that for as long as I lived that I would tell all the other millions of innocent men, women and children in Great Britain the truth!

Yes, I made it crystal clear to him that day, that I was going to tell the whole world the truth of how the British legal system and the British government had abandoned and persecuted my family and the 10,000 other innocent souls that had perished with me. Just because a government was allowed by law to very conveniently *forget that we, the innocent, ever existed!*

I had waited two years for that moment.

Even if he had not invited me to comment, I went into that courtroom with every intention of speaking! I wanted him to know, that he, was sentencing an innocent man and woman!

I was not stupid, I knew that he would not show any concern for me and neither would he support my cause either.

He would never in a million years have joined forces with me to fight for a change in the law to see that the innocent are 100% protected and 100% compensated. But it was my chance to tell him that the law of the UK that he represented stank like a rotting fish.

In truth it stank more than the corpses of the innocent victims that it had just butchered. And I was certain of the fact that for so long as he got paid his grossly outrageous wages he would not give a damn! How wrong the laws in the United Kingdom were!

Yes, I hoped that he felt some pity. I also hoped that he might feel guilty himself, in what he was about to do next.

But I was wrong!

Instead of showing any sign of remorse or feelings for me, my wife and my beautiful sons, and for all our wonderful employees and their families that had all suffered so terribly, he stood up and shook his right fist at me! As his body twitched and his face was bursting like an over ripe tomato, he growled and shouted very loudly, "Take him down!"

So I bowed to him!

Not liking the *cut of my jib*, he leaned forward and almost fell over the front of his top bench, and shouted, much nastier this time, "I said, TAKE HIM DOWN!"

And this time he started waving both his arms like a windmill, beckoning to the bailiffs that stood beside me.

Then he bellowed, with saliva running from his slack mouth, "Bailiffs, I said get that thing," (meaning me), "out of my Court, NOW!"

Those last words from Judge Coleman were spat at me! Again, similar to the night when the High Court Sheriff jumped out of my bushes of my driveway to my home, I was faced again with such childish and unprofessional behaviour by an officer of the law, who really should have been behaving with much more decorum and dignity, that I almost forgot where I was, and I very nearly burst out laughing in the courtroom!

Luckily, somehow, I just managed to restrain myself. Instead I returned his adolescent aggression with a very polite, "Thank you, sir," and another deliberate and slow low bow. And just for devilment I held my out right arm in front of me and I turned and said, "Ladies and gentlemen of this Court of

Justice, Judge Coleman has just made it abundantly clear to us all that he will not be joining in with my campaign to change the grossly negligent laws in this country."

And I added, "I say to everyone in this courtroom today, thank you for coming and I sincerely wish that today you have witnessed an innocent man being found guilty of a crime that he did not commit, and indeed I also hope that today you witnessed history being made, for in finding me guilty, Judge Coleman has proven beyond any reasonable doubt that the laws in Great Britain are shameful, because they do nothing to protect the innocent!"

Finally I added, "Ladies and gentlemen of this court, thank you and goodbye for now!"

It was my sincere aim that day to not let my destruction pass into history silently!

For had I not spoken up for myself and for all the thousands whose lives had been ruined, then surely that would have been the biggest crime of all!

I knew from that day onwards, for the rest of my life, that the fight to change the law in the UK, a fight for true justice, a fight to protect the innocent from greedy banks that go bust, evil receivers and governments that abandon their innocent citizens, had just begun!

My crusade to force the change in the laws in the United Kingdom and in every country in the world that cruelly base their laws on the British legal system had just started.

I never regretted one word that I said that day! My life was now set very firmly on a mission to protect the innocent and there was no dammed way that I was going to be silenced by His Honour Judge Coleman or by anyone else either. I was going to fight to my last breath for the innocent underdog victims of the world!

The greedy banks, the stupid politicians and the law could go to hell as far as I was concerned and there is no way on God's earth that I would be silenced or forgotten either!

Following my verbal assault, Judge Coleman was speechless, he gasped for air like a fish out of water, his face changed colour from a deathly pale white to a crimson blue. The confidence and air of superiority, which he had carried with him when he had so dramatically entered the courtroom only some twenty minutes before, had all gone. He was a blubbering, saliva-drooling, completely out of all personal control wreck, and he dared not say it, but I bet 'have him horsewhipped' were the next words given the half the chance he wished he could have used.

But very sadly for him, and luckily for me, he was 200 years too late, there was to be no horsewhipping that day.

As it was, he just slumped back in his chair, flopped his arms on his bench and looked as though he had just taken a blow in the stomach from one of the burly bailiffs. Then my two minders, ever so lightly touched my arms, turned me and they escorted me out of the court.

As we walked along the crowded corridors of the building, one of the bailiffs did something that I thought was quite extraordinary. He stopped walking, turned to face me, smiled and said softly, "Well done, lad, I have never in all my years seen someone as innocent and as polite as you."

And I thanked him, then the bailiff added, "I believe that I have seen history written today, boy, because you are right in what you said in there, it is the job of the law in this country to protect the innocent, you, your wife, your family and your staff and their families should never have been punished in the way that you have. You are all innocent lad! And I am no solicitor or judge, far from it, but I do have common sense which is more than I can say for Judge Coleman in there!" Then again he repeated himself, "Well done, lad, it's a nasty day for you today is, but I think you will turn out to be all right in the end, I really do! That's what I think about all this and I don't care who knows what I think either!"

And with those words of genuine kindness and compassion, the three of us continued with our walk, deep down into the bowels of the building, where I was led into the prisoners' cells.

In the cells that raining, February, Tuesday afternoon, my pockets were emptied and all the loose change that I had was taken away from me.

A statement was read to me by a clerk about what I could and could not do as a new bankrupt, and I was supposed to feel guilty, but I was not. How could I possibly feel guilty, when I was completely innocent?

When the whole ritual was over, instead of feeling sorry for myself, I thanked the clerk and my guards for their kindness and, in turn, each one thanked me for my cooperation.

In the two years since Chancery's collapse, I had been forced to adjust to a new way of life. On the positive side, now that I was no longer a multimillion pound business dynamo, I had no pressure to perform.

Big business is exciting, but it is all time consuming and demands total dedication, and that was now all gone.

I used my newfound time as wisely as I could. I actually had more time now, for Mandy and the children, and for myself too. With that newly found freedom, I learned how to enjoy golf, reading and going for walks with my family and I had come to appreciate that money alone was not all important! Totally beyond my control my life literally had been changed out of all recognition.

As I left the court building that Tuesday afternoon, I was very poor but on paper at least I was released from the whole tragic Chancery Bank, collapse affair.

I was not punished that Tuesday afternoon. I could still play golf, read a favourite novel, and spend much more time with my fantastic, lovely wife and beautiful children.

So you may be asking yourself these questions, *receivership and bankruptcy*, what purposes do they serve?

Well here is your answer: it gave the receiver to the collapsed bank legal access to my business and my personal wealth too. Simply put, it put them in control of everything that I once owned and it put me totally out of control over any of my lifetime-accumulated wealth.

As for all my past assets and worldly goods, they were now safely in the hands of the receivers and they were now past my concern.

Tragically some years later, I learnt that they had disposed of my entire estate for a tiny fraction of what it was worth. I am reliable informed that they raised just £2 million pounds, that is just 1% of their true worth!

So by cleverly exploiting a loophole in the law, they had forced me, an innocent customer, into receivership and bankruptcy simply because they thought they could do a better job than me of selling off my assets. It was the biggest mistake that they could ever make!

Still the law of this wonderful country allowed them to do what they did to me, to my wife and children, to my employees and, ultimately to their families too! We all suffered, and they, the receiver's had acted legally and guess what? Very tragically I was only one customer of one bank that had collapsed, very sadly I can tell you that the way that we were treated, that other customers that I knew were treated in the same way too!

I estimate that in total that the customers to Chancery, British and Commonwealth and BCCI banks must have added up to hundreds of thousands of people and their collapse must have seriously affected millions of poor sods lives. The human misery caused was on an unprecedented scale. Never before in the history of the world, had so much damage and harm been caused to so many by so few!

We, an entire generation, were *attacked and left for dead.* We were abandoned and we were forgotten!

Very strangely, the human suffering caused to the innocent customers of the fallen banks, was hardly ever spoken about in the national media. The national press and the national media were deathly silent on the subject and all the time that we, the innocent, were losing everything, the Thatcher government did nothing! That is right, they did Sweet Fanny Adams!

Yes, you heard me correctly we, the innocent, got zero protection and sub-zero compensation! As for the circus-like world of the bankruptcy court, as far as the law was concerned, I was now officially free of the whole sad Chancery Bank affair. That affair was now a part of my history!

The piece of paper that the Peterborough County Court issued that day in February 1992, called a Bankruptcy Notice, forced me to let go of my past.

Emotionally, I never did escape the terrible misery that the collapse of Chancery Bank thrust upon me and my family.

Since receiving that first letter on January the 8th 1990, up to the bankruptcy hearing on 22nd February 1992, and for a great many years afterwards, the whole nasty experience left me terribly emotionally, mentally and physically scarred and exhausted too, but as tired as I was, I was being forced to move on.

You know life is a journey and the collapse of Chancery Bank in 1990, is just one little chapter in the book of my life.

And at this point, I suddenly and acutely became aware that I was standing at a crossroads with the map of my life being laid, stretched out before me.

I knew for certain at that time, that I now had two stark reality choices to make: first, I could die, disappear off the face of the earth, give in trying, call it a day, quit or whatever. Or secondly: that I could start all over again.

I chose the second.

One thing, however, was also certain, my life had been changed forever and I was never to be the same person ever again.

Yes, I was resolute in that I would work my way back to the top again, but I was never to be the same happy cheerful person that once I had been. Emotionally, I was deeply saddened by losing my past, with that came a very deep sorrow and a feeling of complete helplessness. My daily life was consumed with feelings of tragedy.

To be truthful, Chancery, their receiver and the law, very nearly broke me completely and they did change me forever.

My nightmares were severe, violent and frequent. Each day when I arose, I felt exhausted and I was either average, not good or, very bad. I suffered terribly with depression.

The internal battle raging in my conscious and subconscious mind between good and evil, light and dark, positive and negative, was with me when I slept, it was with me when I was awake, and it was with me every day!

I can tell you now that those feelings I had every day for a great many years, in fact I would say for around fifteen long years, in all, and I had to live with that.

On the Tuesday after Mandy and I were pronounced bankrupt, I was free, but I was seriously damaged goods! I knew that there would be another day and another day after that. And no matter how bad I felt that I had a duty to Mandy and my five lovely sons to succeed, to be a winner again!

Even though I had my very own Mount Everest to climb, I convinced myself that like the Rocky in the movies and the real Rocky Marciano, who has always been my hero, that for them, my lovely wife and my brilliant sons, that I would pick myself up off the canvas floor of life and that I would fight back to being a business success again!

I convinced myself every day that dwelling on the past was a wasted emotion and that as bad as I would no doubt feel that I would survive!

Driving towards my home from the Peterborough County Court that Tuesday I took a detour. Before I set about the task of rebuilding my shattered life, I had something very personal and special that I had to do.

My dad had just been made the Mayor of a town in north Cambridgeshire called Wisbech, and out of my love and respect for him, I had to put my own personal feelings last and I had to go and see Gerald, because I was so very proud of what he had achieved in his own lifetime! The long journey on the road to recovery was about to begin, after this brief but private pit stop!

CHAPTER 12
THE JOURNEY TO GERALD

My father, Gerald, was born in chronic poverty in the great Depression of 1929 into the poorest Fenland farm worker's family that you could ever imagine.

One of ten children, he left school at twelve to work manually on a local farm. Life for him as a child was very hard and terribly cruel.

To escape that harsh poverty, at just seventeen years old, Gerald joined the army and fought in Africa and Malaysia. After nine years' service, Corporal Gerald Ernest Salter, returned to a village life in Cambridgeshire where he married my mother, Jean. At twenty-six with only the very few pounds of army savings that he had accumulated, he started a tiny wholesale fruit and vegetable business and the first few years were absolute hell.

Between them they worked virtually twenty-four hours a day and seven days a week and it was into that world of constant work, financial and emotional insecurity, that I was born in 1957.

I was to be the eldest son of six children.

So that my mother could have fewer children to look after, my father would take me to work with him and wherever his work took him, I was there. Every evening, every weekend during every school holiday I was always with dad.

I therefore spent thousands of hours with him. I listened, observed and I absorbed a vast amount of information about his wheeling and dealings. I was spellbound when I was in his company. I was sharing time with one of the sharpest truly self-made businessmen of his generation.

I was in awe of him and I still am to this very day. He was a true rags to riches business legend of his time. In fact I would place him as one of the greatest businessmen of all time.

Not that he was the wealthiest man that ever lived, for I am certain that many others were in fact far richer, but I rank him so highly because of the enormous adversity and the chronic poverty that he had conquered and had overcome through complete dedication, self-sacrifice, saving and shrewdness. He eventually made many millions of pounds in his trade and I witnessed it all. All the pain, all the gain, all the gory and the glory.

I have enormous respect for Gerald as a brilliant businessman and as a devoted father.

So the very same afternoon I walked out of the bankruptcy hearing in the County Court in Peterborough on Tuesday afternoon 22nd February 1992, I travelled to Wisbech in north Cambridgeshire, the Capital of the Fens, to visit Gerald to congratulate him on his mayoral appointment, but as I drove the borrowed very old and beaten-up Fiat Panda with a broken windscreen, I did not know if he would be so proud of me. He knew that I had just come straight from the bankruptcy court, in fact I think that the whole population of East Anglia at that time, were fully aware of the story of the collapse of my business empire and I was very nervous to meet the great man!

I felt that I was going to a personal audience with Onassis, Churchill, or Kennedy such was the greatness of the man who was my father. I felt humble, not guilty or ashamed, just humble.

I had fallen from wealth and grace and even though I was not to blame for that, I did feel down.

On arriving at the plush Georgian mayor's parlour, he rushed down the reception stairs to meet me. He looked fantastic with scarlet robes, a white lace collar and his large gold chain of office. At sixty-two years old he was at the peak of his career and I was at the bottom of mine.

I looked drab and formal in my black suit and black tie, and my head was held very low, but I should not have been afraid for upon seeing me, his face was bright and glowing, he was radiant. He held out his arms for a fatherly hug and we embraced.

Then he kindly enquired, "Are you OK, Paul?" Remarkably he was not interested in talking about himself or his new civic appointment, his only thought was of me and my well-being.

I answered, "Yes, thank you, I am fine."

Beaming from ear to ear, he said that he was pleased. Then after looking me straight in the eyes for a few seconds, he winked and smiled and said these extremely kind and very wise words.

"Paul, let me tell you something important, that in all my years in business that I have learnt, failure it is just an imaginary place that we all visit. Never ever give in, Paul. Promise me this, that you will always keep trying and that you will never stop trying! Always remember that one tiny word that I taught you when you were a little boy 'try', it consists of three very powerful letters 't-r-y'. They are so enormously powerful because they tell us that when you try, anything is possible and if you stop trying then all is lost, and your enemies have won. Have your enemies won today, son? Or will you keep trying for me?"

My answer to those extremely kind words of enormous wisdom took a fraction of a second to come from my lips.

"Dad," I said, "not even you or anyone else has any chance of stopping me from trying. Not now and not ever!"

And with that, we embraced and held each other tightly.

I vowed to him that day, as I had done to Mandy that I was never ever going to lie down and die. And he was very relieved to see that I was indeed fine.

But though in front of my father, on the day his mayoral glory and my bankruptcy, I could smile in the face of my adversity, life was tough, very tough and it really was no joke! I had just lost everything and I was frightened to death, for my poor innocent little family!

*

CHAPTER 13
NO JOKE

On the very next morning immediately after the bankruptcy hearing, the receiver to Chancery Bank served another formal demand upon me, by the same cheeky postman, which plainly said: *We want your house now, and we are seeking a repossession order for it!*

Consequently, the days, weeks and months that followed passed by with great fear and pain. We lived from day to day with the very real concern that we would be evicted from our home and that we would be thrown out onto the street with nothing but the clothes on our back that we stood up in.

We loved our family home, it was where our twins, William and Alexander and our youngest son, Harrison, had been born.

The 'Chocolate Box' 1937 thatched house with its leaded windows and the adjoining five acres of paddocks that went with it, was what we had worked and saved so hard for.

We purchased it at the peak of the residential property prices boom in late 1988. Our mortgage on the whole lot was £250,000, an absolute fortune in its day, but at that time we could afford it.

Immediately upon purchasing our home, I succeeded in obtaining planning consent for a massive extension and a separate garage block too, and I obtained consent for the conversion of a former World War Two piggery building into a block of seven stables. The extension and garage were never to happen.

However we did manage to convert the piggeries to stables so that we could accommodate our twin sons' little ponies, which made Mandy very happy because horses to her was her life and to see her sons in the saddle was everything to her.

Horses and competing on them was in her blood. In her own youth, Mandy had been a national child riding star, winning countless county championships as well as major national pony competitions.

Even before they could walk, as soon as the children could sit up in the saddle, they too, followed in Mandy's 'pony riding footsteps!'

And so for a very short while in the late 1980s we lived in bliss and happiness in our detached leaded-windowed, late art deco thatched house set in its five acres of high hawthorn-hedged paddocks in the middle of a nice part of the multi-award winning Fenland village of Wimblington in beautiful rural Cambridgeshire.

The peace and tranquillity of the massive open spaces of the flat Fenlands was my escape from the cut-and-thrust of the business empire that I had forged and created and it was a million miles away from the hustle and hassle of the City of London streets that I strode so often.

Wimblington village was also Mandy's birthplace and it was where she wished our family to live, so that when our twin sons arrived she could be close to her parents in the village that she had spent her own childhood. That was fine by me, a born Fenman and a local lad, for I too, was born into the similar and small Fenland village of Gorefield, not far away from her chosen Wimblington.

But all of that homeliness, peace and stability was about to change. In point of fact, that all changed from exactly 9 am on Wednesday 23rd February 1992, when I opened the *formal demand* from the same cheeky local postman. This was *hand delivered to me* the very next day, immediately following our bankruptcy orders issued on Tuesday 22nd February 1992 by the Peterborough County Court.

So it was that I had to sign for a formal demand, that told me the receiver to Chancery Bank were *immediately seeking a repossession order for our home.* This was no joke!

In plain English, it basically said: *We want your home and we want it now!* So now I was forced into a fight to save our home from repossession. Little did I know then but that fight would last for the next three and a half gruelling years. And it was to be a fight of gargantuan proportions, where I would fight like the legendary 'Fen Tiger' to keep possession of our family home.

And that Wednesday morning, boy was the fight on! For not only did the postman arrive that Wednesday morning, but two other workmen did as well!

By only 10 am on Wednesday morning the 23rd February 1992, two men from David Wilson, Estate Agents of March, in Cambridgeshire, were outside our house banging several 'For Sale' signs into the roadside frontage to our home, in plain view to Mandy and myself, to every neighbour, to every dog walker, every motorist, and to every village gossip, the men were hard at work!

Mandy did not cry, why she did not was a mystery to me, she had every right in the world to be sobbing her heart out, but bravely and resolutely, she did not shed one tear!

When I delicately asked her how she felt, her answer was this: "Paul, I feel numb. I am speechless. I simply do not know how the people who have attacked us these past two years can be so cruel? And promise me, please, that you will fight to save this from happening to us. Please promise me now that you will fight to stop our house from being sold!"

And I promised.

I was angry, not at the workmen that were carrying out their duty, banging the signs into the front of our property, but at the callousness, coldness and vindictiveness of the official receiver who had acted so swiftly only twenty-four hours after our bankruptcy papers had been issued.

So I went out to meet the men working out on the verge. On seeing me walk up to them they smiled kindly at me and held out their hands of greeting.

As I studied their faces, I realised that they looked familiar to me. I was standing before two old friends that I had not seen for the best part of twenty years. Both Chalky White and Nobby Clarke, sign erectors for David Wilson's of March, were pals that I had gone to secondary school with; both were old childhood friends.

Instantly we were reunited boyhood mates that many years before we once were. Both of them then said to me...

"Look Paul, don't be angry with us. We are very sorry and we know how you must be feeling right now and the whole town and district know what happened to you and Mandy and about the bank that went bust, but David Wilson sent us here and he said to give you his best and kind regards. We are to tell you that he had got a telephone call at nine o'clock this morning from some bloke in London and that we are to put the sale signs up straight away, without fail!

"So David said to tell you that we are just following orders from this bloke in London and he told us that we had no choice and to get on with the job."

Both the lads that I knew from my schooldays were good honest, down-to-earth, Fenmen and both were deeply embarrassed and ashamed to have to carry out this duty.

Without any doubt I knew that this act of brutal immediate action and aggression had not come from any East Anglian man. That would never have been the case because in our rugged rural part of the world a man's word is still his bond and he conducts his life by very old-fashioned, codes of conduct of chivalry, honour and duty.

No, this master plan to take immediate and very public action upon me and my family was organised by an outsider and by one who had very cruel intentions, too.

During the building up of the property empire that Chancery and their henchmen had so cruelly taken off me, I had done many years of great and excellent business with every estate agent in every town and city in East Anglia and David Wilson of March in Cambridgeshire was one of them.

Guessing what the attacker's theory, hopes and desires were, I vigorously shook the offered honest hands of my friends, patted each one on the back, smiled and said, "There will be no 'For Sale' boards going up here today, boys. And boys," I said, "under any other circumstances, it would be great to see you both, you know that, but these signs come in off this Highway verge now!"

And I added, "Look, they may have made Mandy and I bankrupt yesterday, but they have not won any eviction order yet." Then I read them the receiver's document of that day. "All this says is that they are *applying* for an eviction order," and I let them read the document. Then I looked them both straight in the eyes and said, "The London receiver who telephoned David this morning has no evection order yet! What he *hopes to achieve* is to get an offer from a member of the public who see these boards and then he will go and ask a judge to throw us out of our home. And I say that is wrong! And I will not allow that to happen to my family! We have been hurt enough by these receivers who hide behind the small print of contracts and who use the law to their unfair advantage. From this day onwards, this family makes a firm stand against such tyranny and we will not be evicted until a judge fairly grants a proper eviction order, and that will be after we have presented our case as to why we should not be thrown onto the street.

"And until such time as a proper eviction order is granted, which over my dead body, God willing, it never will be! My home is not 'For Sale'!"

And with that I pulled all five sets of signs up out of the verge and put them back where they had come from, straight into the back of Chalky's and Nobby's small lorry.

"Oh and," I added, "when you return to David, give my warmest and kindest regards too. And boys, be sure to tell him that I may be wounded, but that I ain't finished yet!"

And with that news, both Chalky and Nobby left me. They knew I was no danger or threat to them, us Fen boys always stick together. Neither by the same token was I upset with David Wilson, but both my boyhood friends knew that I was deadly serious, bitterly angry, and very hacked off with the way that an outsider was treating my wife and children!

Following their empty handed departure down the road, I went inside my house and telephoned my previous business solicitor, Jan Limming, at Billings and Peterson, of Park Road Peterborough. Even though she was kind and calm on the telephone, I knew by years of experience of dealing with her that Jan was disgusted too at the very hostile way the receiver was treating us.

The threatening and bullying of our family went down like a lead balloon with Jan, for these were the identical extremely aggressive and non-negotiable tactics that had been used originally on January 8th 1990 when I was give no proper time to save my companies when the same receiver completely ignored the assets that they were holding as security against the loans, made by the collapsed Chancery Bank of London, and demanded instead that I repay them the whole amount in full, in cash, in just twenty-eight days!

Now for the second time, they were using their bully boy, strong-arm tactics to force an immediate sale of my home even when they had no fairly won eviction order.

This time it was not just my companies' assets that they were after, no. This time it was much more personal. They wanted the roof over the heads of my wife and little children. And whatever value there was in our home they wanted it immediately! They were putting enormous pressure on our family.

Jan's belief was that they would apply to the courts claiming that under the personal guarantees that Mandy and I had innocently signed to the stricken Chancery Bank, which stated that in the extremely unlikely event that the bank itself went into receivership that they could ignore the sale of my company assets, demand that their loan be paid back in full in cash in just twenty-eight days, and if I failed to repay them in cash within twenty-eight days that they could put my companies into receivership and apply for our bankruptcy, and upon our joint bankruptcy, that they would demand the immediate sale of our home.

Amazingly, Jan kept her emotions and anger under professional control then she said, "As a favour to you and Mandy, Paul, I will fit you in at eleven o'clock tomorrow morning. And Paul, do not be late, bring Mandy and oh Paul, do please bring that scrap of paper that you were served this morning with you. Oh, and do not worry about the cost either, this one is on me!"

The following morning both Mandy and I arrived promptly at Jan's office in Peterborough. We duly handed her the receiver's document and watched her expression as she read it.

"Ah hah! Just as I thought, they are trying to bounce you both and your trustee in bankruptcy too! Let me explain my dears," was her motherly response. "Am I correct in assuming that neither of you have ever been in a situation like this before?"

To which both Mandy and I said, "Yes that is correct, Jan. This is entirely new territory to both of us."

"Very well," she exclaimed, "then neither of you will be aware that you will soon have a trustee in bankruptcy appointed by the court whose sole job it will be to liquidise and deal with all your personal affairs, all your assets, your savings, your investments, the benefits of any kind. Your stocks and shares that you own, any antiques, works of art, jewellery, everything, including the sale of your home.

"That trustee will work very closely with all the receivers to your former companies and see to it that your creditors are paid back as much as is humanly possible, and this whole procedure will take time." Then she paused, winked and grinned. "If the penny has not dropped yet, Paul, let me pose a scenario. What if your former companies get broken up and sold off for a massive profit, who gets that money after each of your creditors are paid off? Why of course, it is your trustee in bankruptcy." She chortled. "And with all your former development sites and building land assets it could take years to sort the whole package out, and," she continued, "now let me propose another scenario, how much is your mortgage now on your home? And who do you have your mortgage with?"

To which my reply was, "£250,000 to the Nationwide Building Society."

"OK," Jan continued, "and in today's chronic recession racked market what do you think your pile is worth?"

To which my reply was, "Probably only £125,000."

"Right," she said loudly, almost jumping in the air, "we have at least two factors here that will see off any repossession order. Well for some time at least. First, you have substantial net worth in your former companies and Chancery Bank are not the only creditor, nor is their receiver the only receiver appointed to your former companies by your various other former banks, but in fact they represent the smallest lender and creditor that you had. So they therefore rank way down the list as a low-level creditor, and very importantly, in the current climate, you have what we call *negative equity* in your house.

"That is where the current value is substantially lower than the amount that you have borrowed and where in any event, the lender is not Chancery Bank but Nationwide Building Society.

"Given these factors alone, any reasonable judge would not hurriedly grant a repossession order now especially to the receiver of Chancery Bank and will most probably not do so either for some considerable period of time, and that my dears, could be several years!

"No I am convinced of it," she said boldly, "given the vast size and worth of your massive companies which realistically could see all your former creditors paid off completely and given the negative equity now that you have in your home, especially one that has the first charge on your home, not to Chancery, but to another lender who is passive and not aggressive, any reasonable judge will permit you to stay in residence while the several other receivers to your former companies and the trustee appointed by the courts themselves get on with their business of selling off at the highest price that they can, your former assets. And the Nationwide have proper time in which to sell your home and the receivers to Chancery Bank who rank very low in your list of highest ranking creditors, will not get their wicked way!

"My very strongest advice to you my dears, is to hold on tight and stay put. Let us befriend and work with your trustee in bankruptcy, for they will not be bullied into taking hasty action. And as you have no money at present with which you can pay me to defend you, let me see if I can get you some temporary Legal Aid, because keep attacking you Paul they will, I am certain of that!

"For my theory is this, the receiver to Chancery Bank believes two things: first, that you are both stupid and that you will take any ridiculous deal that they put to you to sell your lovely home, probably to someone that they know and they then offer to go away and leave you and your family in peace and second, that you have no one like me to defend you!

"Well, let me tell you Paul and Mandy, they are bloody well wrong on both assumptions!"

Then Jan leaned forward, smiled, and said, "Now, go home to your children and leave this nasty little receiver to Chancery Bank to me!"

And by the tone of her voice, the twinkle in her eye and the smile on her motherly face, I knew that Jan was in control and was enjoying every minute of it, too!

CHAPTER 14
SERIOUS HEALTH ISSUES

The journey home from Jan's office that Thursday afternoon was happier than the journey that we had made to her in the morning.

Mandy and I felt a tad more comfortable that our family would not be repossessed straight away. We often speculated where we might all end up if things came to the worst. Truth is we simply did not know what our fate would be!

More cheerful now that Jan was going to fight our corner, we pulled into the driveway of our home to be greeted by Doreen our friend, our three fantastic sons and our white Retriever, Dudley.

My re-occurring thought when I saw all their innocent happy faces waiting for us was 'how could human beings act so cruelly towards each other', irrespective of what the law says or what this clause allows you to do. How could people act so terribly towards each other?

Garry, my faithful brother-in-law, Mandy's only brother and I, had travelled to London on the same day that the very first formal letter had arrived to say that Chancery Bank had gone down and we journeyed there with good faith in our hearts and a willingness to do everything that we could to assist them.

Only when we arrived at their London head office we were rudely received, bluntly turned away and told to see our solicitor. Why could their official receiver not negotiate with us? He could have at least had the decency of talking to us nicely.

Since January the 8th 1990, I must have asked myself these questions a million times over. Strange when I say that line, that catch phrase 'a million' it keeps popping up and coming back to haunt me. For it was exactly a million pounds that I owed the bank and that was the reason why the official receiver could not be nice, it was because he was demanding that sum of money!

And to him, Garry and I were not people, we were amounts that he intended to collect as his small print allowed and as a result we were insignificant and he did not need to be polite; he did not have to talk to us and there was nothing to negotiate under the text of the guarantees that Mandy and I had signed.

He was due his whole amount back, in cash, in twenty-eight days and that was final, he had no need or desire to talk, period. After all, the law in the UK was on his side, and he knew it!

This may sound incredibly simplistic but I believe from the 8th of January 1990 that the official receiver to the bank was a robot trained in his profession by another robot and that was that. There was never to be any friendly talk and there was certainly no kindness towards us on his part and there were absolutely no feelings for us, there were no emotions, because he was programmed to have none!

In fact, I believe that any sign of care and consideration on his part would have been seen by his bosses as being a sign of weakness!

They say that history repeats itself, I hope that is never true in this case, but heavens above should it ever be, please Lord, program these receivers with a little more feelings for their fellow mankind. For talk and friendliness costs nothing and is directly opposed to nastiness, litigation and non-negotiation which causes misery and costs a fortune!

Good kind behaviour is the way that I have always done business and with kindness and cooperation, I have made many millions of pounds and I have moved mountains. Attack and bludgeon to death tactics only brings fatality which in my case, fatality almost became a reality!

For only twenty minutes after arriving home with Mandy on Thursday 24th February 1992, I collapsed with a suspected heart attack. I can vaguely recall hugging the boys and thanking Doreen for looking after them, while Mandy and I had to go on our urgent business to see Jan at Peterborough, but after that I remember nothing else.

What I next clearly recall was very strange. I was in the operating theatre at the hospital and I remember floating to the ceiling, looking down at my body and seeing the team of doctors and nurses working on my lifeless form. I could hear them talking to each other and they were panicking.

I felt no pain, only a warm feeling of happiness and contentedness then nothing else!

Some hours later, I awoke in a hospital bedroom. I had wires on my chest, a tube up my nose and a needle and drip in my arm. Above my face and shining a light into my eyes, was a doctor, he had three nurses with him.

Sitting beside my bed and holding my left hand was Mandy. She was crying, her head was buried on my hand and I felt her tears wet my skin.

Something beeped near my right ear, it was the heartbeat monitor.

Then I heard the doctor say, "Thank God! We have got him back!"

I learnt later that I died in the operating room and several times in the intensive care ward! But by a miracle, the hospital team had revived me and kept my very weak heartbeat going!

Unable to do any more for me, they were forced to keep an around-the-clock watch over me while they awaited my fate.

The doctors who cared for me, told Mandy that I would probably not survive the night and that realistically all hope was lost! Even so she insisted that she would hold my hand and that she would pray for me. As for God, he had decided that he would let me stay for a while longer, probably just to be a nuisance to the receiver to Chancery Bank and he returned me to the land of the living!

I stayed on in hospital for a full two weeks. To this very day, I believe that the heart attack was caused by the stress of the collapse of Chancery Bank and the horrible persecution of our family by their receiver.

The combination of these factors had taken its toll on my health and it had very nearly killed me!

Visibly I had lost over three stones in weight. I now weighed barely eight stones instead of my normal eleven and a half. My dark curly hair had mostly fallen out and what little remained was now grey.

My nose and teeth would often bleed and my no-smoking lungs coughed up blood. I needed pills to sleep and pills to wake.

When I did sleep, the nightmares were so bad that I screamed and often hit out and punched Mandy, awake or a sleep, I could not escape the daily onslaught.

Almost every day we received another demanding letter from Berkings Solicitors saying how much interest we owed on their clients outstanding debt or how much their fees were that I owed to them. Because under the guarantees that Mandy and I had both signed to Chancery Bank, we had agreed to pay their costs too!

Consequently, the letters from Berkings kept coming through our front door like confetti and all the time that they dropped on our doormat, their fees kept escalating. Every letter Berkings could write to me was pushing the amount that Berkings were owed, higher and higher and higher!

Basically, Berkings were earning more and more money for themselves the more the action that they took against our family and then as Jan would say, *the penny finally dropped!*

I was so naive that it took me a while to see what was really happening to us. My unfortunate situation was a gold mine, for the jackals who very happily picking at my bones and who were charging and earning a fortune for themselves from my misfortune.

The receiver and their henchmen were having a time of their lives earning their fat juicy fees from me and they revelled in writing to me daily and by being as nasty as they could. They earned their excellent living by being as litigious as possible. The more they wrote to me, the more fees they were due.

The pressure was endless and was never, ever going to stop until they killed me, which they almost did!

Now at last I knew the truth as to why the receiver turned Garry and I away that day, when we arrived on his doorstep in London on the afternoon of Monday January the 8th 1990. To him, we were already dead meat and we were the biggest and juiciest feast that he probably ever had all his life. We were a wounded and dying beast and like the vulture that he was, he would stand on top of us and pick our carcass clean!

CHAPTER 15
DIRTY WORK

In early 1992 I was alive, redundant and I did not have a clue what I was going to do next!

Thanks to Jan Limming we still had a roof over heads, but I had no income with which I could feed my family and so I begged the only businessman I could find for a job, his name was Benny Gold.

Benny was the original Arthur Daley, if anyone alive knew of a scam it was Benny, expertly streetwise, Jewish and sharp! Benny knew all the angles.

To look at him you would think that he was a penniless tramp. His long grey hair curled out of the back of his old threadbare and battered blue berry. His seventy-year-old face was always unshaven and his clothes looked as though he had slept in them for the past six months, which he probably had!

Added to which, even in the depths of winter, he wore his slippers in his paper-strewn, littered and rundown unheated office. He resembled and acted like Fagin after a very bad night out on the town.

Typically when I asked him for a job, he rubbed his hands together and said, "What is in it for me?"

And my reply, as honest as ever was, "Mr Gold," I said, "I am broke, I have no money, nothing! But if you can find me a job please, I will do any work for you that you ask me to do, and sir, my life is indebted to you, if you help me now in my hour of greatest need. I will never forget your gratitude!"

And so Benny took me to one side and told me all about cleaning toilets.

Benny ran a small-time car boot sale at 'The Posh'.

'The Posh', as the locals called it, was the football stadium for the Peterborough United Football Club. On Sunday mornings their car park was used by car boot sale sellers to display their unwanted second-hand domestic goods, and it was my job to keep the toilets clean!

The toilets were abused badly every Saturday when 'Posh' played a game at home. The paper towel and toilet paper litter in the loos was beyond description and smell of the urine, vomit and stench of stale beer in the gents' loos was a rank stench that you would never forget all your life! And the ladies' toilets were always in a far worse condition.

You could not blame the Football club for this abuse of the toilets, it's just that when you get many thousands of toilet users relieving their bowels and bladders during a 90-minute game that bad smells will always result and littler will accumulate.

And on a Sunday morning while I was picking up the assorted refuse, the sounds and odours that surrounded me was disgusting.

Sick, shit and piss smell fantastic first thing on a Sunday morning!

But I had a job as the Sunday morning car boot sale toilet cleaner all for the princely sum of £5 per hour. And when the loos froze in January 1993, guess who had to dig the shit out of the pans? You guessed it! Me!

Twelve months after my apprenticeship, Benny called to me to his office. "Hey Paul," he said, "Charlie, the car park guy has just died. If you want, you can do that job, pay is the same but at least people don't piss on you!"

I took the job, but Benny forgot to tell me about the rats!

When Benny had offered me Charlie's job, I innocently thought that it was a reward, a promotion of some sort. Little did I know that I was wrong! It was just another crap and stinking occupation that no one else wanted to do!

So in early 1993, I was knee-deep in litter from the aftermath of the Sunday morning car boot sale that Benny ran surrounded by my new friends – the rat family!

Benny's idea of cleanliness was to leave all the day's rubbish in a refuse skip in the corner of a car park until the rubbish cart came along to collect it on a Thursday, by which time, all the wild animals for twenty miles around had had their fill, and that is why Benny's lovely business premises was infested by rats, whole dynasties of them!

Still a job was ten times better for me than no job at all. At least I had a purpose in life, something every week to look forward to and to me, when you have no purpose to live, you are dead!

And as horrible as the work was, I was grateful for it!

Through my darkest hours, the jobs that Benny gave me kept me alive. I knew that if I kept working that better times would come again. I also knew that if I ever gave up trying that I would die!

CHAPTER 16
LIVING ON THE BREADLINE

Living in poverty is not easy, it is to say the least, very uncomfortable and unpleasant. The very few pennies that we received from the government, due to our extremely low income, on income support and the few bob that I gathered on a Sunday from Benny meant that we had to be very skilful how we spent the precious little that we had!

Once upon a time, it had been normal to go into a supermarket and buy what you wanted, that was now no longer an option. Before the collapse of Chancery Bank we could book a holiday abroad, we could visit a cinema, we could travel to the seaside for a day out, we could buy a magazine, we could have a meal in a café and the children could have a toy.

Well, all of that was now ancient history and none of that was possible. What you could spend, where you could travel, what little treats you could afford, were really big issues!

Suddenly the most important things in life were the basic requirements for survival: food and heat topped the list by far.

Clothes could now only be old, worn and second-hand, holidays did not exist and all luxuries, however little, were banned.

The degrading jobs that I was doing for Benny Gold, the sadness caused by signing on at the dole office every other Tuesday morning in my small home market town of March, in

Cambridgeshire, and the taking away of my entire financial freedom, made me very hungry for new success.

I was so hungry, that I was ravenous!

In fact the hardships that had been imposed upon me during the early 1990s, made me more determined and angry than anything I had known all my very hard life.

Yes, I was angry, not just at the way that I had been abused, but I was truly furious at the terrible hardships that my beautiful wife and children had to endure. Due to the collapse of a London bank, the law in the UK fully supporting their receiver and a government that had abandoned us! Boy was I angry!

I was very angry for the terrible suffering that my innocent family were being put through and I was angry too, for the hundreds of thousands of other innocent men, women and children who had lost their businesses, their homes, their jobs, their life savings, everything when the three London banks of British and Commonwealth, BCCI and Chancery had gone bust.

We were all innocent and helplessly caught up in the entire bloody mess! We were all innocent victims caught up in a national disaster, the likes of which recent modern man had never known. And we were all legally robbed!

The truth is that Margaret Thatcher's government did not care about us; otherwise they would have come to our rescue. They should have protected us and compensated us for every penny of our losses, yet they did nothing!

My firm belief to this day in 2012 is that the government could have come to our rescue but they chose not to! Instead they simply decided to abandon us, to not talk about us, to quietly forget us and, hope that we would die and go away! We were all attacked and left for dead and in time we would be completely forgotten! This was Thatcher's cheapest way out.

Instead of our rescue, our abandonment was the option that her government chose to take. Guess what? in 2012 you are still dangerously vulnerable because there are still no laws that guarantee what happened to us, *will never happen* to you!

Make no mistake about it, in 2012, you must fight and demand that new 100% protection and 100% compensation laws are passed now in the UK, and in every so-called civilised country of the world, because until they are passed, no one in the world is safe! Simply put, you must fight to have your campaign heard, because while we were being massacred, the government was silent!

I state clearly now for the record that I believe that the hidden and the forbidden *real truth* is that the Thatcher government found it cheaper to ignore us and to abandon us! They simply decided not to protect us and not to compensate us either for the billions of pounds that we had lost when the three major banks in London went bust and when the receivers to those bust banks came for our homes, our life savings and for all our worldly possessions too. In fact, they stood idly by and watched it all happen!

We the innocent customers of the banks that had gone bust should have been protected by our government, we should have been protected by the British law and we should have been compensated for our losses. Every penny in our businesses and savings should have been safe. Instead we were not to be rescued and we were expected to be lost and forgotten in history!

And now in 2012, as you read my true story of what happened to my family, you should be terrified for yourselves!

The law must be changed and you the innocent must be protected now!

Yes, I was very angry then, but there was nothing that I could do about it. I was alone and I was desperately trying to survive. And now in 2012, I am angry for your sakes, too!

I sincerely hope and I pray to God that history does not repeat itself!

But in 2012 with the chronic state of the British economy and the extremely serious trouble that surrounds the banks in the UK and around the world, it worries me greatly that this misery and human sacrifice will indeed happen all over again!

And to prove my fears to be *correct*, ask your current government to change the law and to give you 100% protection and 100% compensation when the next bank or banks go bust, and see what answer you get!

Ask your current government to protect your home from being repossessed, ask your current government to protect your businesses, ask your current government to protect all of your life savings and your jobs, and let me know the answers that you get back!

In 2012 there still are no 100% protection laws and no 100% compensation laws and until there are you are in very serious danger of losing everything, make no mistake about it!

Your campaign for a change in the laws in the UK and elsewhere around the world will be a fight of gigantic proportions; expect the politicians to give you clever words, slippery promises and false smiles and expect your campaign to protect your families, the ones that you love and everything that you have ever worked and saved for to be the biggest and most bloody fight of your life!

Your right to be *100% protected and 100% compensated* when banks collapse are very real serious issues and it does not matter a fig if you come from England, Northern Ireland, Wales or Scotland, America, Australia, Portugal, Greece or Timbuktu. It does not matter a jot if you are black, white, brown or green, it is irrelevant what religion you worship or if you have no religion at all. And it matters nothing which political party you support!

Because your campaign to give you *100% protection and 100% compensation laws* affects every person, from the very richest to the very poorest, on this planet! In the UK and in every country throughout the entire world, when banks go bust and while there are no laws to *100% protect and to 100% compensate you*, until then, you are all doomed!

It is time now for you, the innocent in the UK and throughout the world, to rise up, speak up and to defend yourselves!

Always remember this, if the governments in the UK and those around the world have nothing to lose then they will gladly give you what you ask for, won't they? And they will gladly give you your new *100% protection and 100% compensation laws* now in 2012, when you need that protection most!

Well, we shall see!

Until that change in the law comes, let me continue to describe to you in graphic true detail, what daily life was really like following the collapse of Chancery Bank of London, following the forced receivership at just twenty-eight days' notice of all my companies and following the forced bankruptcy of myself and my wife by the receiver to Chancery Bank.

We were so poor and our family was so hungry that I had to scavenge Benny Gold's rat-infested skips for rotten vegetables and potatoes with which I could feed my wife and children! Also I did errands for the fruit and vegetable stallholder that I met on a Sunday morning at the Peterborough United Football Club car boot sale.

I would beg for food, I would grovel, I would remove his smelly empty boxes and rubbish all day long and I would sweep his pitch clean for him when he left the site. In return for which I was given items that were rotten and unsaleable; that is how we survived!

I was so poor that I could not afford to buy the freshest vegetables, let alone buy the freshest fruit! As for meat, this same process was repeated; I would beg, grovel and clean for the market butcher at the 'Posh', I scrounged the out-of-date meat that was probably going to be dumped at the end of the day: decaying chicken legs, liver and kidney was the weekly nutrition for my family!

All the meat was so near its 'sell-by date' that it was discoloured and produced bad odours. The luxury of fresh meat we could not afford: steak, joints and chops were completely and for now permanently off the menu! Only fresh sausages and a small bag of mince were our occasional luxuries!

This was what 'living on the breadline' was like for my wife and children and myself in the early 1990s, and I was determined I would change all that.

I vowed to Mandy that we would not spend the rest of our lives eating rotten vegetables and 'gone off' meat from Benny Gold's Sunday car boot sale!

Do not get me wrong. Mandy and I were both eternally grateful that Benny had given me a job! In reality, had he not been so generous then I do not believe that we would have survived those years: the low cost food; the little pay and the ability to work kept us alive! But this lifestyle took a very serious toll on my physical and on my mental health too and I had to escape from it or die!

I had become horribly thin, my rib bones stood out against the tight skin of my body and I had become terribly lonely and reclusive! In fact, I spoke very little and never smiled, I just kept my head down and solemnly went about any task that Benny gave me!

But as grateful as we were, I could not carry on cleaning out foul toilets, loading filthy rubbish into vermin-infested disposal skips and begging for rotting food forever!

Things had to change because that lifestyle was slowly killing me!

CHAPTER 17
THE BUSINESS TENANCY

During the early 1990s, Jan Limming, of Billings and Peterson, of Peterborough kept the roof over our heads. She succeeded in getting us Legal Aid from the Law Society, and that paid for her expenses.

Chancery Bank's receiver's solicitors, Berkings of Slough, continued to produce a mountain of recorded delivery threats and they must have been responsible for the total destruction of at least ten rain forests. While this was going on, despite a slowly recovering property market, Nationwide Building Society still had enormous negative equity in our home and the pittance from both Benny Gold and the Income Support cheques, kept our family afloat, just!

The receiver would still not talk and be pleasant to us. In fact, he took us forcibly before three separate county court judges on three wonderful and memorable occasions, doggedly-determined and desperately trying every legal and almost every non-legal trick in the book to secure a repossession order on our home.

Each time Jan came along to court with me, every time we returned home victorious and on every occasion the official receiver went mad when he did not get what he wanted! He hated not being in control and, worse still, he was a very nasty and bitter loser!

Coming home from every victory in court, Jan would council me, always her advice was the same: "You do know that one day, Paul, that nasty little man will beat us and get a repossession order, don't you? Because not even I can hold him off forever," and then she would always burst out chuckling in a motherly hen, kind of way. But her message, despite her joviality was never lost on me, I knew just how high the stakes were, and that one day soon we would lose our home!

But lucky for me the receiver to the fallen Chancery Bank worked alone in his quest to see Mandy, I and our three beautiful sons thrown out on to the street!

For all the other receivers to my previous companies were still fighting each other over my corporate corpse and their in-fighting and squabbling was literally giving me time to live and breathe, as for Mandy following the birth of our youngest son Harrison, she decided to continue to teach the children of our village to ride.

She took over the running of 'The Wimblington Riding School', that her mother had first started on the land to the rear off our home in 1962. That riding school had been run continuously by Mandy and her mother for over thirty years, originally operated on land owned by our predecessors and then since our purchase in 1988, on the land owned by ourselves.

The club had around forty members and it had a committee too. Also the club had its own bank account and it kept proper annually audited accounts, also it kept all the receipts for the purchases that the club made and that included receipts for the rent of the fields – our fields – that the club used!

When the fact of Mandy's occupation and the history of the independent 'Wimblington Riding Club', came to the attention of Jan Limming, she almost did a somersault with delight.

She told Mandy and I, "You do realise what you have innocently permitted the riding club to have, don't you?" she said. "You have only entitled the club to have their own business tenancy on your property and," she continued, "as you now tell me that you also very generously permit the members of the club to come and go with their cars, stock, materials and all their horse transport, straight through your garden to your home too, on a seven day a week basis. You have given the club historic rights of way over the gardens of your home."

To which Mandy and I innocently answered, "Yes, that is correct. The Wimblington Riding Club do pay rent for our fields and, yes, it is also correct that we do let the members come and go as they wish, through our garden, so as to gain access to this land in which they ride, which lies at the bottom of our garden."

And Jan remarked, "You confirm that you give signed receipts for the rent to the club."

We answered that we did.

"Well," she said, "this is all fantastic news. Without knowing what you have done, you and your predecessors have granted the riding club both a *full business tenancy and historic rights of way,* that legally permits them to occupy the fields that you own, which the club has used without interruption for the past thirty years, on land which they, the Wimblington Riding Club, have continuously paid rent and on which they have committee records and receipts for and, what is more, you have also innocently given the Wimblington Riding Club a vitally important historic right of way straight across your private dwelling driveway and your garden too."

Jan continued, "So let me tell you now, Paul, what all of this means as far as the law is concerned, innocently you and Mandy and your predecessors have given the Wimblington

Riding Club both a legal business tenancy of your land and a legally protected right of way, so that their members can come and go whenever they wish, seven days a week, 365 days of the year through your garden and the law of this country will fully protect and preserve, those tenancies and their very well-documented historic rights of way!"

Then she added, "I have no doubt about it, the club have cast iron legally protected rights and if you wanted to get them off your property you can't! *So you, Paul and Mandy, are stuck with the club!"* And she almost fell off her chair with laughter!

"Therefore until those rights are removed, your home has a business tenant which makes it virtually unsaleable to anyone else! For who else in their right minds would want all the comings and goings of the club coming right through the middle of their front lawn and even if a repossession order was granted on your house, the rights that the Wimblington Riding Club hold would still be protected by the law of this wonderful country!

"So Paul, your house and fields not only has a sitting tenant, it has a seven day a week transport route right through your driveway and gardens, which is more of a bloody nuisance! I am certain of it! There will be very few purchasers for your property that would put up with the disturbance and nuisance caused by the coming and goings of the club members with their cars, horseboxes and lorries!

"Beyond any doubt, in my professional opinion, the long-established thirty-year-old, Wimblington Riding Club have established and proven *legally protected rights*! And I am 100% certain that those rights will be protected by the law of our wonderful country!

"This puts the club in an extremely strong position. Therefore Paul, this is very important, you must ask the

Chairman of the club to contact me immediately! Because in addition to representing you, I am now going to represent them as well! I will stop their historic legal rights being taken away from them!"

And so it was that I did as I was told, and I got the Chairman of the Wimblington Riding Club, to speak to Jan Limming!

CHAPTER 18
I ALMOST GAVE UP TRYING

During the early years of the 1990s with our home under constant daily threat of repossession, I had my battered pride, a job with appalling work conditions and very low pay, and that was how we lived!

The Wimblington Riding Club, together with their forty or so members had a business tenancy over our paddocks, together with a right of way through our garden and their committee was legally represented by Jan Limming.

The months ticked slowly by and we were forced to adjust to our new way of life. Even more slowly, I began to think about the future which made my sore head hurt for I was not sure any more what the future held for myself or for Mandy and our children

My foggy brain painfully started on autopilot to observe the world around me. My business instincts were not completely erased, even though in truth I was a very seriously beaten and bruised human being!

Despite this fact, the gift of inquisitiveness that I had been born with, still somehow managed to function. Here and there, I started to see tiny opportunities for making a little extra money while I was working knee deep in trash and rats!

I observed that people would throw away unwanted goods that could be sold again for cash and I was not too proud to scavenge!

To get to the point. I had fallen to the lowest level in my life, I was quite literally *in the gutter* and I was surrounded by dumped filth and rubbish, doing a job no one else wanted to do, and my self-esteem had sunk to such a level, that I did not care of what people thought of me! I was up to my waist in waste picking up anything that could be salvaged and sold again, from the skips of Benny Gold's Sunday car boot sales, and it was from that position that I started on my journey on the long hard road back to financial recovery!

As I went about my duties at Benny's boots in Peterborough, when the public and the stallholders had vacated the Sunday car boot sale, I stayed on for several hours to pull the skips apart and by carefully sifting and inspecting the trash, I put to one side anything that could be sold, even if it would only make a penny. This is how I started to make my next extra cash. When I returned to work the following week, I would offer my newfound treasures to the car booters as they arrived on site and they kindly purchased my goods from me!

As a result of my efforts I got my new stock for free and every penny that I made was pure profit!

My new little enterprise bought me in an extra £5 to £10 per week. That small amount made a world of difference to my *positive mental attitude* over the following months!

Slowly I began to regain my self-belief. I saw that given time and great patience that I could quite literally drag myself out of the sewer. By selectively sifting through other people's discarded junk, and selling their unwanted items for a small profit, I could be born again.

As the song says, (Dorothy Fields/Jerome Kern) I knew there and then *that I could pick myself up, dust myself down and start all over again!*

As a very little boy I had come from complete poverty and, through my own efforts, I had risen to make a 200 million pound fortune! The secret to that success was based on observing opportunities, following a plan through and saving every penny that I earned!

So I started my own *micro-scale* waste reclaim business. Within just one month I had saved the vast sum of £50! Within two months I was selling reclaimed stock and buying extra stock with my savings off the car boot sale stalls. Within three months my savings had risen to £100!

By the early spring of 1995, I had earned £1000, and by the summer of that year my savings totalled a staggering £5000! And it was then that I said goodbye to Benny as an employee and instead I became a *full-time* Sunday car boot trader, on a never-to-be-missed basis!

Oh, but I did not say goodbye to my good friends the rat family because I continued to scavenge through the garbage every Sunday afternoon!

During those years, from time to time, I kept in touch with Jan. Every time I did speak to her she, like a doting mother, reminded me *that I must do something permanent about securing our home,* but that was easier said than done!

Of course it was my most cherished desire to own again our own home! However, there were several fundamental problems that had to be overcome before the dream of re-owning our home again could ever become a reality.

To start with until February 1995 I was a bankrupt, so getting anyone to lend to me was impossible because as a bankrupt I was forbidden by law to have any form of a loan whatsoever that included, of course, having a mortgage. And secondly, there was the other plain fact that I had no proper job either! Being a 'Del Boy', wheeling and dealing in reclaimed rubbish and other cheap second-hand goods on a Sunday car boot sale, was hardly going to win me any new friends in proper building society either!

So despite Jan's well-intentioned good advice, there was bugger all I could do about purchasing our home off the Nationwide Building Society that I still owed a quarter of a million quid to!

Still by February 22nd 1995, my bankruptcy was over and overjoyed with my new freedom, it was in the months that followed that I naively and stupidly made the biggest mistake of my life. Out of sheer inquisitiveness, I telephoned the Nationwide Building Society and asked them politely that if I could find myself a willing lender, would they sell our home back to me?

Innocently, I asked them how much money they would want for our freehold.

Knowing very well my precarious circumstances, they acted nonetheless very gentlemanly and kindly to me. Amazingly, they offered to send a chartered surveyor out to inspect our home, to see if a valuation could be arrived at and to see if the matter could be amicably settled once and for all and the chapter could be closed in their book!

I thought at the time that, like me, that they were getting tired of the whole sorry saga but I could not have been more wrong!

Within a few days they sent along their surveyor and a few days after that a settlement figure was produced. We had purchased our lovely home in its five acres of grounds at the peak of the property boom in 1988 for £250,000. Now some seven years later and still in the depths of the most severe recession ever known to modern man, the Nationwide Building Society were willing to sell my property back to me for the amazingly low sum of just £61,500!

I was speechless! Of course I knew that the property market was chronically sick and, to be frank, at that time in history, property still had virtually no value.

The country under Margaret Thatcher had been bought to the verge of bankruptcy. There was mass unemployment and stagnation on an unprecedented scale, the whole nation was paralysed! In fact Margaret became so unpopular with her colleagues that she was soon to be forced out of her stronghold of Number 10 Downing Street in tears, by her own political party.

Britain like its banks was bust!

But could it be true, could the Nationwide be so realistic? Could it really be so straightforward? Or were the Nationwide playing me at a game? I soon found out the answer to my thoughts.

Unwittingly, I had just walked into the biggest trap in my life! Yes, on the face of it, I could now buy back my home for only £61,500, but I had no new willing lender. What had started out as a pure and simple exercise by me, a few weeks earlier when I requested a theoretical settlement figure, ended up leading me into the biggest nightmare of my entire life that far!

Because within a few days after their offer to sell to me, the Nationwide Building Society themselves, filed for a repossession order for our home! It was suddenly *put up or shut up* time! Quite literally I could buy our home off them or get out of it!

This time the court hearing for the repossession order would be entirely different to those that had gone before as the mortgage provider themselves were making the application. This was not the receiver from some unrelated source.

This was not the nasty little receiver from Chancery Bank, who were entirely unconnected with the loan on our home. No! this time it was the prime lender themselves, the Nationwide Building Society, asking a judge to give them back their property, which they owned and which was occupied by our family.

Added to this the Nationwide, for their part, had been seen to act so reasonably by letting the purchase price appear so realistic.

Given these facts of life, according to the advice of Jan Limming, it would be grossly unfair of any judge to not give them the repossession order to our home, and I was stuffed, big time!

In the early summer of 1995, for yet another time in my life I received a knock on my front door! This time it was a formal demand from my mortgage lender, the Nationwide Building Society, to pay them £61,500 in cash in twenty-eight days or get out of their home. And I had to sign for the safe receipt of that formal demand!

Once again, I had twenty-eight days *to piss or get off the pot.* No willing new lender in twenty-eight days or get out!

Mandy, my three little sons and myself were guaranteed this time to be made homeless! I was, and I felt, completely trapped!

I was a recently discharged bankrupt; I had no proper job either, at least not one that was a bankable proposition. It was true that after I was discharged from bankruptcy on 22nd February 1995 that I started as a self-employed market and car boot sale operator in my own right, and that my prospects were looking the brightest that they had been for many a year, but I was not a candidate that any mortgage lender would welcome as a customer.

As for Mandy, she brought precious income into the household each week, as she continued with her riding lessons for the children of the Wimblington Riding Club. However she was not a bankable proposition either!

It was then that I panicked! How the hell could I come up with the £61,500 in time? Damn how I hated those *twenty-eight* day clause rules!

Frantically I stopped everything else I was doing and picked up the telephone to every high street lender that I could think of and, you guessed it, not one, and I mean *not one* was remotely interested in helping me!

Damn! How I hate déjà vu!

Not one company was interested to lending to an ex-bankrupt, with no steady job.

I also contacted every business person that I could think of from my past, not a single one of them were interested!

So I did something highly dangerous and risky. I contacted every unsavoury loan shark that I could think of too, knowing full well that I was showing great weakness to the most dangerous of men who armed with the knowledge of my perilous situation could so easily have waited for the Nationwide to win their repossession order and then approach them direct themselves for a deal!

And guess what, not one Great White Shark was interested in lending me any money because with my unsavoury record, I was judged to be too hot a risk for them to handle too!

Also at this point in time you must remember that Nationwide had been sitting patiently and waiting for over five and a half years for the property market in East Anglia to recover. Which it did not! Everyone and, I mean everyone, was petrified of lending to the collapsed property market in East Anglia!

Also when I had to reveal to any possible lender that our home *had a sitting business tenant on it and a right of way over our garden*, every person that I spoke to said very firmly, "Sorry, we cannot help you!"

I was buggered. I had no willing lender. I hated to admit it, but I was beaten! No one that I could think of would come to our rescue.

I was desperate and I was exhausted. It was at this time that I almost gave up trying!

Then it was Mandy that came up with a suggestion. She stated that we should ask a distant relative that she had, who was a life assurance broker, if he would assist us and help us find a mortgage.

That man was Peter Reeve.

I thought that she had gone mad! Peter was newly widowed and newly self-employed. To be honest, I thought Mandy had lost the plot, I thought that it was madness, especially because Peter was a life assurance broker and he was not a mortgage provider. However I privately decided to play along with her suggestion to speak to Peter, if only so that I could state to her later that I had followed every possible opportunity through. Even though her idea was crazy!

When we met Peter in the mid-June of 1995, we had less than fourteen days to go before we were ordered to appear before the County Court in Cambridge city, for the Nationwide Building Society's repossession hearing.

Peter was charming, polite and brutally frank, which are virtues that I admire in all men. I hate rudeness, I detest time wasters and I loathe bullshitters!

So from the beginning Peter and I got along just fine! But there was the major problem. Peter had never arranged a mortgage before in his entire life!

What had started out as being a half-baked idea by Mandy, now touched on the fringe of lunacy! Nonetheless Peter said that he would try and help us. He was serious and genuine and I had no other option but to let him try. He was our last and he was our only hope!

At a guess I would say Peter was of a solid grammar school education, very middle-class, quite tall at almost six feet three inches, and as straight as a die.

His light grey pin striped suit, matched his grey shirt and tie and his grey socks and shoes, his dress sense, like his lifestyle, was safe, smart and sound.

My belief was that there were no hidden vices or skeletons in Peter's cupboards and what you saw was what you got. From the very first meeting Peter was charming, friendly, warm and comforting; he always had a bright kind smile and an air of thoughtfulness and respect for Mandy and myself.

"I will try and help you both," he said reassuringly, "but you must be patient and trust in me that I will do everything that I can to find you both a lender. But please do not blame me if I cannot deliver."

"To be honest," we told him, "without your help, there was no hope left." And we let him get on with his task and we prayed to God that Peter could pull off a miracle!

While we waited for him to perform, Mandy and I visited Jan and asked her for assistance. But Jan could give us no comfort at all.

"Mandy and Paul," she said, "I feel terribly sorry for you both, I really do, but your time has come, you are finished. Any judge that this application goes before will rule that given over five years of waiting, given that the Nationwide have offered you a wonderful private sale at a figure substantially below what you originally borrowed from them, that it is only right and proper that you and your family should get out of their mortgaged dwelling. I am very sorry, but this time you have no defence. A repossession order will be granted to Nationwide Building Society and you are out!

"Oh Paul, by the way, do not think for one minute that a judge will give you any more time to live in your home, make no mistake about it, Nationwide have waited patiently these past years and they have treated you and your family very well indeed. The judge will give you no more time, you will not get one second longer!"

I felt gutted, but I was not surprised at her honest opinion!

On Wednesday 28th June 1995, the day for the hearing in Cambridge County Court arrived and I was ordered to appear. The stage was set for 2.30 pm that sunny afternoon!

Jan Limming could not come with me. She had announced *that it was a complete and utter waste of her time and that she had other urgent business that she had to attend to,* so I had no one to defend me, only myself.

Mandy, who is a leading equestrian judge, was already booked to appear at a national horse show at the East of England Showground, at Peterborough, so she could not attend the court with me either. She was taking the children with her to the pony show, Mandy and the boys were all camping on showground for the duration of the four-day show and she begged me to forget going to the Cambridge Court and join them to make a holiday of the children's pony show, but I could not.

In the twenty-eight days since receiving the recorded delivery demand from the Nationwide, I had eaten little and I had slept even less.

The very thought of having a happy time with her and our children and knowing all the time that we were now being officially made homeless, with nowhere to go, make me feel physically sick. So as my beautiful wife and three wonderful children left home with the children's faces smiling at me and with Mandy looking extremely worried, I prepared to go to Cambridge to meet my maker.

On the train to Cambridge, I telephoned the ever cheerful Peter Reeve to see if there was any hope on the horizon at all of receiving a formal offer of a mortgage from a willing lender.

As they say in the Fens of Cambridgeshire, *I was clutching at straws!*

At this last moment, I believed in my heart that if I could produce to the judge a faxed piece of paper, to say that someone or other was willing to lend me the £61,500, that he would take pity on me and give me a little more time to perform.

There was, of course, no certainty that the judge, whoever he or she was would do so, but I had to try.

To my total amazement, Peter did not disappoint me. He said that until twenty-four hours ago, he had tried everyone that he knew of and that no one would assist. However, he had just come off the telephone that minute to the Kingston Building Society and they felt that they might be prepared to do it, but that their fees were not going to be cheap!

To the surprise of my fellow passengers in the railway carriage that June morning, they saw me, a grown man in a smart suit, dance, shout and scream and run around the train compartment like a mad crazy fool!

Upon regaining my composure, I said, "Peter, I do not bloody care how dear their fees are, just get me a formal offer, and Peter, get me it NOW!"

And on the morning of the court hearing, he did just that. Never having obtained a mortgage before in his entire professional life, Peter Reeve brought home the bacon!

When I arrived at the court just after midday on Wednesday 28th June 1995, the clerk to the court handed me a fax and it read perfectly, on Kingston headed paper, it said the words to this effect:

To whom it may concern,

*We the Kingston Building Society are prepared to advance the sum of £55,350 for the purchase of the property...
(The letter stated my address in Wimblington.)*

It was a letter that offered me, subject to contract and to survey, a 90% mortgage. I was ecstatically happy!

All I needed to do now was to persuade the judge and the solicitor for the Nationwide Building Society, to give me another *twenty-eight days* to complete the legal documentation from the Kingston Building Society so that I could transfer the title, from the Nationwide Building Society, to the Kingston

So I still had a mountain as big as Kilimanjaro to climb. Before the court sat at 2.30 pm I had to clear my head and to prepare for my presentation because I stood completely alone now. It was only the strength of my presentation before the judge that could save our home, this was make or break time!

If I fumbled, mumbled or made a hash of my presentation, to the judge, I knew that all would be lost!

So with two and a half hours before I had to appear in the court, unrepresented before the judge, I walked about two miles or more through the streets of the University City of Cambridge, one of the most beautiful cities in England and a place that I love so much.

As always the traffic was busy and even though it was almost their summer holidays the city was full of young students on bikes. I have always found Cambridge city to have a happy feeling, of youthful hopes, dreams, romance and love!

And that day as the sun was shining, there were no clouds in the clear blue sky, only mine, for I was on cloud nine.

At ten minutes to two I informed the Clerk to the Court of my case number and of my arrival, also of my intention to represent myself.

In the past five and a half years, I had been in so many different courts in so many towns and cities that I understood the *court etiquette* as well as any solicitor or barrister.

The tall middle-aged bespectacled clerk in the billowing jet black robes duly wrote down on his large bundle of red-ribboned papers my name and details.

Within a few moments he had spirited himself away inside the closed doors of the court to deliver the news of my arrival to his fellow clerks and bailiffs, who awaited me.

On the stroke of two thirty, the heavy oak doors of the courtroom were thrust open by two beefy ushers and I was told to enter.

The four of us stood and waited at our prearranged positions, frozen to the spot in total silence.

Apparently the judge was still at his midday lunch break, probably in some dining room housed within the exceptionally fine Georgian building.

The next five minutes seemed like five years. Then the same clerk came silently towards me and in a whispered voice told me kindly, that I was to sit down now and that he would get me to rise when it came for my turn to speak. He also mentioned that the solicitor for the Nationwide Building Society was not yet in attendance, but that fact would not stop the hearing from proceeding.

As the hand on the courtroom clock clicked to precisely 2.35 pm, the same clerk announced, "All rise for his most Worshipful Judge Simmons!"

Everyone in the courtroom stood to attention in reverence to the incoming judge.

Judge Simmons then appeared. He was a cheerful looking, portly man I guessed in his late middle-age, with white curly hair and a slightly reddish plump face.

He crossed the high bench before me. He deliberately nodded to all present in the court and sat down. Then he spoke and in a very quiet, kind and calm voice to me said, "Mr Salter, you are here before me today alone, I believe."

I said as politely as I could, "Yes I am, Your Honour."

"Very well," he added, "at least you have had the courtesy to come to my court. However," he continued, "I have received notification from the solicitor to the Nationwide Building Society to say that he unfortunately, could not attend due to unforeseen circumstances. A fact which I find very irritating, as surely any reputable firm of solicitors have a great many staff and one of them could have represented their client in my court. However be that as it may, he has asked me to grant a repossession order for your family home and, even in his absence, I will still have to consider his request on the merits of the documents that he has presented to me.

"Mr Salter," he continued, "as I understand it you offered to purchase your home from the building society, did you not?" And with those carefully chosen words he lowered his head and gazed at me over the top of his half-moon glasses waiting for my reply.

"Yes, Your Honour," I said, "that is correct, I did make such an offer."

"And," he continued, "am I correct in believing that you have failed to arrange finance to take up their offer to sell you their property?"

This time my answer was slow and clear. "No, Your Honour, that is not correct." And with that I put out my right hand and held out the flimsy piece of faxed paper from the Kingston Building Society.

The clerk of the court strode across the courtroom floor to where I was standing and took my limp sheet of A4, to the judge, who studied every word, full stop and comma on the almost transparent sheet. The next two minutes passed like an eternity.

With my breath held and with my heart thumping inside my chest I waited for his next words.

"Mr Salter, I must commend you for coming to my court today even if you do represent yourself, which if you ever do again, I will treat you harshly for, however, through your persistence you have proven to me today that you have not failed to secure an offer of finance to purchase your home from the Nationwide Building Society, therefore it is impossible for me to grant an order for repossession today in their favour.

"Instead I instruct this court that you be given another twenty-eight days to produce the finance that the Kingston Building Society has offered you, and it is my instruction to the Nationwide Building Society that they fulfil their offer of a sale to you. However," he continued, "should you fail in your attempt to conclude this arrangement in the next twenty-eight day period, then I state for the court records, that the Nationwide can come back before me and petition for your repossession and I will grant them their order.

"Do I make myself clear, Mr Salter? I am giving you another twenty-eight days to close this transaction otherwise I will grant the order to the Nationwide."

At this point I smiled to the judge, I told him that I understood him perfectly and thanked him on the behalf of my wife and three little children.

With our business of the day finished, Judge Simmons arose and walked off the stage that he commanded.

And at that moment, I was a very relieved, happy man!

CHAPTER 19
THE LONG ROAD TO RECOVERY

Mandy was judging ponies and riders at the East of England Showground in Peterborough and she was in the centre of the show ring in full concentration of choosing the best turned out pony and rider. She had no mobile telephone on her so I could not contact her to tell her my news.

Also Peter Reeve was on answerphone, no doubt he was out on business somewhere and Jan Limming was very busy with clients and was not to be disturbed. Therefore on the telephone outside the County Court at Cambridge on that victorious and glorious day in late June 1995, I did not have a soul in the world that I could tell my fantastic news to!

Even though the distance between the courtroom and the railway station was a short distance, I did not walk back to the railway station in Cambridge that brilliant sunny afternoon, I floated, my feet never touched the ground! I felt as though I had just won a million pounds on the football pools!

Instead of stopping at March Station I continued on the train to Peterborough and on my arrival, I paid for the balance of my fare. Then I boarded the Number 47 bus for the East of England Showground.

As the double-decker trundled on down Oundle Road that early Wednesday evening, I could not help but to remember that it was over five and a half years since I had received the first letter on 8th January 1990, from the receiver to the collapsed Chancery Bank of London giving me just twenty-eight days to perform!

And here I was now being given just twenty-eight days again to perform by Judge Simmons of Cambridge, but at last, I felt that I was travelling along the long hard road to recovery, or so I hoped!

On arrival at the East of England Showground, I eventually found Mandy in a corner of the massive 300 acre showground and she was amazed to see me.

"What are you doing here?" she said. "I thought you were going home and that you would telephone me tonight at 8 pm as we had arranged."

Then she froze where she stood and began to visibly shake with terror and said, "Oh my God, Paul, it has all gone wrong, hasn't it? We have lost our home!"

When I carefully held her hands and told her everything that had happened that day, she collapsed in a heap on the floor and passed out cold. As gently as I could I carried her in my arms into out borrowed horse lorry. She was clearly mentally and physically exhausted!

When she came awake she started to cry, she was sobbingly uncontrollably! It was abundantly clear that the strain of the eviction order and the fear of my self-represented court appearance, had been weighing very heavily on her mind.

So I held her as tightly as I could, I kissed her hair and I told her we had won that day. And then she cried even louder!

Exhausted myself, that night I slept the very best that I had done in years, in the tent with our children, still dressed in the suit that I had worn for Judge Simmons.

The following morning at 6 am I awoke and went to the shower block nearest to our camp to wash. Then I kissed

Mandy goodbye and walked the four miles to Jan Limming's office, in Park Road, Peterborough.

Luckily there was no rain and the early morning birdsong lifted my spirits to a height that I had not experienced in a very long time.

I arrived at 8 am a full hour before the solicitor's office officially opened. I knew that Jan liked to be first into her domain and be ready for the day's action before her junior staff slouched in.

I rang the front door bell and on seeing me unshaven and untidy in my crumpled suit standing on her doorstep, she very nearly repeated Mandy's actions of the night before.

"What's wrong?" she said, and then, "Oh my God! You are homeless aren't you? You poor wretch! Do come on in and let me make you a cup of strong coffee and you can tell me how it went yesterday."

As she usually did, Jan sat completely still and silent and digested every word that I told her. When I was finished she simply leaned across her huge red leather-topped desk and held out her arms and hugged me.

Beaming, she said, "Well done Paul. I am so very proud of you!"

It was very clear to me that over the many years that we had done business together that Jan and her staff had become much more to our family than just business associates, we had all become very close friends and what is more, we were friends that had no secrets.

"Right," she continued, as soon as my bunch arrive at nine o'clock, we shall begin straight away to get the new mortgage moving with the Kingston and, Paul," she said, "I promise you this, our staff will use all their best efforts to complete this transaction within the time that Judge Simmons has allowed or, they will have me to answer to!" And she added, "Paul you can go and comfort Mandy and tell her from me that should we fail in our task, I will personally come with you to see the judge to ask for even more time, however, you have my cast iron assurance that it will not be necessary to do so.

"And for further reassurance," she continued very seriously, "Paul, I vow to you here and now that we will move heaven and earth to see this transaction through!"

And by God, she meant it!

Then she continued, "Now I insist that you go back to Mandy and enjoy the pony show with your children. Oh and Paul, you are not walking back to the showground, I will get Tracey, my secretary, to take you in my car."

And with that I went off to see my family.

Now at long last I felt both safe and content, in fact by only 9 am that Thursday morning, my work for the day was done.

The weeks that followed came to a conclusion two days before my twenty-eight days were up. All went well, but we hit a last minute major setback. And when I say major, I mean very major!

Jan telephoned my home and in an unusually agitated voice she said, "Paul, I have good news and I have some very bad news for you, which do you want first?"

Being accustomed as I was these past few years to only hearing bad news I said, "Just for a change, Jan give me the good news first."

So Jan explained her dilemma. "The good news is that the money is ready to be transferred to us from the Kingston. Once it is paid into our account, we can release it to the Nationwide Building Society and your deal is completed. However, we have hit a fundamental problem with the Kingston, the Kingston Building Society will not assist you and buy your home until the claim for the business tenancy and the protected right of way are dropped by the Wimblington Riding Club. The Kingston are demanding a clean title otherwise the deal is off!

"I know that this is a new departure and that it has never been raised as an issue before, but I have personally spoken to them today and they are adamant, no removal of the tenancy and rights of way means no money and no transaction!

"I am sorry, Paul, you have no choice in the matter. You have this one last task that you must perform if you want to buy your home back.

"You must persuade the members of the Wimblington Riding Club to drop their tenancy of your land and to drop their rights to go back and forth through your garden, or the deal with the Kingston is off!

"And if you fail in that task within the next forty-eight hours then the Nationwide will go back to Judge Simmons, tell him that you have failed to raise the money and you and your wife and children are homeless!"

I was gob-smacked! The curse of the collapsed Chancery Bank was fighting me back again with a vengeance!

And once again I was back under enormous pressure to perform.

All I could think of saying to Jan was *fuck it*! But I bit my lip!

CHAPTER 20
THE FINAL HURDLE

I had come so near to success. I had defended for five and a half long years, wave after wave, after wave of attacks from the receiver to the collapsed Chancery Bank of London. I had lived every day all those years with the very real threat of eviction.

I had seen my little children grow up, I had seen them off to school, I had read them their bedtime stories and I had kissed their little heads good night, and all the time I had pretended that nothing was wrong.

I had told little white lies to my wife that I had everything under control, when all the time exactly the opposite was true.

In the stillness of the night and in the early hours of the morning when they were all asleep, I was wide awake and worried to death!

Sometimes the pain in my heart was so bad that I would go downstairs to the kitchen for a glass of milk and sit there on my own, alone, with my worries for hours.

Living all those years with the daily threat of eviction was a terrible burden, it had taken a terrible toll on my physical and my mental health too, and it had very nearly literally killed me!

To this very day, I am certain that it was only the wonderful love of my wife and children and a couple of genuine caring friends that kept me alive. I never did feel suicidal, although if I had I fully understood why that would in fact have been a very normal feeling.

What I did feel very much though, through this whole tragic affair was abandoned, alone and I was exhausted.

One of the two close friends that I just mentioned was Jan Limming, the other was my mum, and both had been absolute saints!

But even Jan admitted to me now that she was only mortal after all!

For the first time Jan told me that the many times that we went together to court to defend an eviction order, she was never certain that we would win!

During the five and a half years from January 1990 to June 1995, the worry of eviction haunted me and the fear of losing the roof over our little angels and Mandy's heads nearly drove me insane!

And now Jan was asking me to climb one last mountain, and it was a mountain so high that I did not know if I had the strength left to climb it, but make that climb I knew that I must!

The task that was now before me was almost impossible to achieve. I had to beg the members of the Wimblington Riding Club for mercy. I had to ask them to sign away all their legal rights to our property that they enjoyed and I had just over twenty-four hours to do it all in!

Knowing extremely well the committee members of the club I did not know, if it could be done.

The Wimblington Riding Club was formed by my mother-in-law, Margaret, in 1962. Its sole purpose was to teach children and adults of all ages and capabilities to ride, the club members numbered around forty men, women and children who between them owned twenty ponies and most of those were kept at our paddocks.

Practically all of the members were village or local townspeople who, unlike us, had no land themselves on which they could keep their ponies.

As a result I had to plead with them to give up their historic legal rights to keep their beloved animals at the fields of our home. And I knew they would be devastated, if the club was to be disbanded and if the ponies were evicted! I knew that they would not find any other local grass fields with hedges to graze in. From my local knowledge there was absolutely nowhere else for them to go and that as a result their ponies would have to be sold. The children and the parents of the club would be heartbroken!

The committee and riding club members were a very close-knit community they were fiercely loyal to themselves, their children and to their animals. Very early on in this true tragic story they had banded together and formed an official action group. They called themselves SWRCFE – save Wimblington Riding Club From Eviction – and despite appearing to feel sorry for Mandy, our children and myself, they had thought only of their own legal and historic rights and of their own survival!

Ironically after Jan Limming herself had offered to protect them from eviction from the repeated attacks of the receiver to Chancery Bank, they became galvanised into a commando-like task force with a determined mission and they actually sang, 'We will not be moved' when they attended one of Jan's meetings.

Consequently what Jan and the Kingston were asking me to do now was to break that solidarity and to ask the committee and the members of the riding club to permanently give up their legal rights to the occupation of our land and to their historical rights of way through our property!

Since 1962 to 1987 the club had rented the land from our predecessor and from 1988 to 1995, they had rented the land from myself and Mandy, so for thirty-three continuous and uninterrupted years they had occupied and enjoyed their paddocks and knowing every individual in the club. I knew that they would not give up their historical rights without a very fierce fight.

And now I had a little over twenty-four hours to conclude the deal!

Good heavens, I thought, *my life never seems to get any bloody easier!* It certainly was: *shit hit the fan time!*

CHAPTER 21
THE GAMBLE

In all my life I have never been a gambler. I have always believed that money comes too hard to waste it and to let someone else profit from your weakness is not my idea of having a good time!

99.9% of all people have vices, but thankfully gambling was never one of mine. That was until now.

When I left Jan's Peterborough solicitors' office that day I knew that I had no choice, there was no time left. I had to take an educated gamble and there was just *one tiny timid little lady* that could possibly be the ace up my sleeve!

Like it or not, I had to gamble on the outcome of a frail bullied little lady who might just turn the actions of the lynch mob to my advantage. There was no other way and I had to act fast and hard! And I had to take the chance, that my theory was correct!

Using my latest technology mobile telephone, I called every parent whose child was a club member. For those people that I could not contact, I left messages. And where I could not leave a message I told those that I spoke to spread the word.

I needed to meet everyone at our home that evening. I told everyone that failure to meet would result in catastrophic circumstances that would affect the very existence of the club.

So with that ultimatum I set a time of 7 pm for them all to meet at my house for the news that would shock them to their very core.

By 6 pm the riding club families started to arrive. Mandy gave them tea and biscuits for the adults and orange juices or lemonade for the children.

At the stroke of 7 pm I spoke to those that had come and who were crammed into our living room. Many of them, especially the children were sitting together on the floor, the children were giggling and playing. The adults, however, looked and were all deadly serious.

I was more frightened to stand up and talk before them all than I think I had ever been at any of my previous board meetings in the City of London because basically every person in our room was a very dear friend. And what I was about to ask them would affect each one very deeply!

"Good evening, and thank you all for coming tonight," I started nervously. "Tonight, Mandy and I are going to ask you for your help and kindness." I continued. "Most of you here tonight know that over five years ago that I lost my business due to a London bank going bust on me and all of you know that since January 1990, our family has fallen on very hard times.

"What most of you will not know, however, is that I have nearly lost this house too, and the land that goes with it on several occasions. Jan Limming, our solicitor from Peterborough, that you all know has fought hard for us and has managed to date, to keep the roof over our heads.

"However the time has now come when Jan and I have the next twenty-four hours to save our home or lose it forever!"

There was complete silence in the room, even the children realised that something very serious was wrong and they started to cry.

Very red-faced myself and feeling physically sick, I continued, "In the next twenty-four hours this house and all its land will be repossessed. It will be taken away from us and we will be homeless and, you the members of the Wimblington Riding Club will be the next to face an eviction order."

At that moment the members of the Riding Club erupted like a volcano, the children were all sobbing by now and the adults started to shout at me like a drug-crazed angry mob! They all stood up and started to shout at me! That was everyone except for one tiny frail lady and she was my gamble! She was my 0.01% chance of success, if she performed for me, as I prayed she would, then I would win this battle!

I asked them politely to sit down and listen to what I had to say. This was the moment that I had planned for and it was a trap that I had set and it was now that I was to see if my guess would work or not! Because this frail little lady was the wife of the biggest British troublemaker in the room!

And so I continued, this is word for word, what I added next.

"Every one of you here tonight are our very dearest friends, and your friendship is extremely important to Mandy, myself and to our children. Many of you have been members of the Wimblington Riding Club for all your lives. The riding lessons that Mandy gives to you all bring enormous happiness to the children and the adults too. The annual shows that you hold here I know are very special to you all and on a happy note, tomorrow, all of this can continue forever, because Mandy and I have the ability to buy back this house and its five acres of paddocks from our current building society!

"If we can achieve that, with your support, Mandy and I will give you our word that your club can stay here for all time! Your club can continue to enjoy the use of our paddocks for many years to come and you can all stay here on a completely free of charge basis too. And in future years to come, there will be no more rent to pay for the use of our fields.

"However, to make that happen, what I need you all to do is to come with me and Mandy at nine o'clock tomorrow morning to see Jan Limming at her Peterborough office. You will be asked to sign away your historic legal rights to use our field and the historic rights to come and go through our garden." I then paused for a brief moment so that I could try and gauge the reaction of those present, which was difficult to do as the room had descended into complete silence.

No one spoke.

So I continued. "I am very sorry to say that this matter must be concluded promptly tomorrow morning at 9 am or the transaction with the new lender, the Kingston Building Society, will be lost. And I am very sorry that you were not given any more time but the request from our new lender, only came to Jan this morning and the transaction has to be finalised tomorrow."

Again I paused so that this news could sink in slowly.

Then I added, "If the transaction is not concluded tomorrow then we and our family are out on the street. And you as a club, are off to court yourselves. You will all have to pay to defend yourselves too. Which means not only paying for Jan Limming's bills but for the professional services of a top London barrister to represent all of you in court.

"I am very sorry, but there are no other choices open to us all. You are either with me and Mandy and we guarantee you a wonderful future here together, or you must fight for yourselves and take your own chances in the courts which will cost you, according to Jan herself, tens of thousands of pounds!

"Let me assure you of this. If you support Mandy and myself, we will never abandon you. We will always protect you, and the Wimblington Riding Club will exist forever! But as you can appreciate from the Kingston Building Society's point of view, when they pay off our current mortgage provider, the Nationwide Building Society, they must have a clean and unencumbered title to our property!"

They sat dumbfounded gazing at each other as if they were paralytically drunk, with no one saying anything meaningful, so I repeated again:

"If you all come with me and Mandy tomorrow morning, I vow before Jan Limming herself, that Mandy and I will give you our solemn promise that the club will continue as normal for now and forever!"

And that was that, I could say no more. The decision concerning their future was now entirely in their own hands and I had done my very best to make them see it our way.

I knew it was a gamble and a very risky strategy but there had been no other option open to me.

Jan had convinced me that if the club went against Mandy and myself, then Judge Simmons would evict us and, as always, in this whole sorry saga there was no time left to dilly-dally.

And now the gamble that I had set up and waited for developed before my very eyes. It was at that precise moment that the most difficult person in the room that I knew would be the spokesman for the troublemakers, Steve Smith, a grossly overweight local bricklayer, stood up and shouted his abuse and unwittingly became my greatest asset and saviour. This was the moment and this was the nastiness that I had anticipated and my ace card was his timid and tiny little wife Mary who studied his whole performance, like a hawk.

I knew if anyone in the room was going to be the most difficult, unreasonable and troublesome, it was going to be him. But if there was any person in the room that could outmanoeuvre him, it had to be her!

Appealing to Mary was my only hope, but I was not sure if in fact it was a lost cause because she hardly ever spoke and I had never known her to have an opinion of her own, let alone stand up to her 'bully boy husband'. But Mary, if she could subdue Steve was my only hope for salvation, and she did not disappoint me! She patiently waited for her husband to blow his top and then 'she' went on the attack!

When Steve launched into his verbal onslaught, you must remember that 'nicely put' Steve Smith was a bully! He was a giant of a man who would constantly shout foul language and verbal abuse at his own children and at his timid little wife too!

And like it or not, this is what Steve said, "Paul and Mandy, no one in this room gives a fuck for you! You are in a fucking mess because you could not manage your business properly, it has nothing to do with that bank going bust in London, that is just a load of bollocks. I speak for everyone here and I say to hell with you both! And we as a club will fight fuckin' anyone. You both think that you are fuckin' clever, well you are fuckin' wrong 'cause we have all met in private and we do not give a fuck for you two or your kids either!"

As I looked around my living room all the other adults and children were hiding their faces behind their hands. They were all terrified of this swearing monster, that was everyone except for his tiny thin little wife, Mary, who sat staring at Steve behind her frail wire-framed glasses.

I knew how nasty he could be, and to use his bad language in front of the women and children in the room did surprise me! So now all I had to do was to wait to see what the mob, that Steve Smith was the ring leader of, would do next.

On the face of it, my gamble of getting everyone together in my house was backfiring on me. The evening appeared to be a public relations disaster. I knew that it would have been safer to meet each riding club member individually, but I did not have the luxury of time to do that.

The Kingston Building Society had played their own hand brilliantly and had put me under enormous last-minute pressure. Their late insistence that Jan convey to them, a picture postcard thatched detached property set in five beautiful acres with a clean title was a stroke of pure genius!

The sub-prime lender of the Kingston Building Society was using my position of desperation to clean up the title to a very valuable asset. They were advancing me a tiny sum to get their own hands on a very prime piece of real estate, in actual fact, the Kingston were very cleverly achieving something that the terrier-like receiver for Chancery Bank had failed to do, they were getting control of my private assets for themselves and for a rock bottom price too. It was a 'very smart' move on their part.

Because if I delivered them what they wanted and thereafter if I defaulted on their new mortgage, they could repossess my home themselves and, this time it would be free of any tenancy! It would be free of any encumbrances and it would all be theirs and be ripe for the selling!

All of this, of course, was a gamble the Kingston were willing to take unless I performed, which thanks to man mountain, the bully boy Steve Smith, on the face of it, at least, was looking very unlikely.

But what happened next was to shock me much more than the use of Steve's swearwords. In fact, the events that followed in the next few minutes were actions which changed a life. And that life was ours!

CHAPTER 22
THE DEAL

In my very many years in business I have found that almost always in life when two sides meet and talk, there is a good chance of deal. Nine times out of ten a way forward can be forged between willing parties. The only time in my life when there had been absolutely no way to reach a deal was with, yes, you guessed it right, the official receiver for good old Chancery Bank"!

Despite that one occasion, all my business life I had been blessed with possessing three very fundamental facilities for success: first I never underestimated an opponent, and second: I knew more about an opponent before going into battle than probably an opponent knew about themselves. Third: I always appreciated that a rival needed to survive. So I always gave them the ability to do so in any negotiations. Therefore whenever I went into business battles, I always undertook extensive research into the men, women and situations before launching an attack.

And even though the Kingston Building Society had sprung their last-moment surprise trap for me, I had known the members of the Wimblington Riding Club for many years and I therefore knew the strength and weaknesses of every individual, in particular I knew those who were on its committee intimately.

So when Steve Smith launched into his foul-mouthed attack upon Mandy and myself, I was not surprised at his behaviour. I had seen him behave in that way many times before, although not in front of so many women and little girls and boys.

Steve was a big strong man, an ex-weightlifter, in his prime he was fit and physically awesome, but now in his mid-forties he was grossly overweight and many chinned. His massive bulk bullied smaller, weaker creatures, he enjoyed frightening men, women and children. He was a foul-mouthed yob with no politeness or etiquette! He revelled in his own boasting and his self-importance. He was a heavy drinker of strong spirits both day and night. And his high blood pressured bloated face and swollen hands were deep red and tinged with blue.

Instead of speaking, he shouted and instead of thinking, he acted bluntly. He literally was like a raging bull in a china shop!

When he stood up before the packed room that evening, and proudly declared how he had held many secret meetings with the other members of the Wimblington Riding Club, I was not surprised in the least. In fact I had expected as much because if there was going to be a ringleader among the group, I knew that it would be him and he did not disappoint me, he had proven my theory correct.

Now was his moment of glory or so he thought and he went for the bait 'hook, line and sinker'. So I stayed mild and meek and I simply listened to his ranting and ravings and proceeded to let him play himself right into my hands.

That evening at my home, I was so proud of Steve's unwitting performance. For about fifteen minutes he never stopped talking about how he was going to do this, about how he was going to do that, about how he was going to fucking fight this person, then about how he was going to fucking fight that person, about how he would crush that person then he would smash that person to pieces.

After that, he would kill that next bastard and when he had killed them; how he would kill some other fuckers. By the time he had finished his victory speech, all the children in the room were in tears and my enemy hand just handed me victory on a plate!

Had I roughed it out and argued with him that night I am certain he would have resorted to violence because that was the only way that he knew how to act! Offer to fight him with your fists and he would be so happy to oblige because he knew that by using his brute strength and his fat body that he would beat to a pulp most ordinary statured men.

But to ask him to be sensitive to a crowded room full of women and little children and a couple of mildly spoken little men and he was completely out of his league!

In his own very small-minded way he used his strength and size to totally domineer every meek person in that room and, unintelligently he thought, that by imposing his own bully-boy tactics upon those he believed he was the master of, that everyone would follow him.

In fact he had just made the biggest miscalculation of his life! The women in our living room went across our wood and carpeted floor and surrounded Mandy and started to cry even louder and the children rose to their feet and hugged their mothers' skirts and trousers and they started to sob their little hearts out too.

Big bully bragger and boaster, Steve Smith had just frightened them all to death. Yet incredibly it did not end there. After several minutes of the children and women wailing, Steve started another mad tirade.

"If you silly bloody fucking lot are going to support Paul and Mandy after all we have discussed and planned, then I will attack you stupid soft bloody lot as well!" he bellowed. And he continued, "Go on, let Paul and Mandy lose their house, let us see them thrown out on the street, it's all they deserve! It's Paul's own fault, he did not manage his fucking business better when he had one! They need a good lesson of what it is really like out there. I say they should get everything they deserve!"

And then he played his master card. "Right you lot," he shouted above the cries that were getting ever louder, "who is with me?"

At that precise moment, as if waiting for the cue, Steve's timid little wife Mary stood up and she stepped forward from where she had been silently sitting on our sofa, and in the centre of the room, watched by everyone, she pointed her thumb of her tiny right hand and calmly said:

"I am with Mandy, Paul, William, Alexander and Harrison! And you, Steve Smith are on your own!"

Everyone in the room gazed in silent amazement, and watched and waited, not knowing what was to going to happen next.

What actually happened, in fact, was nothing.

Steve Smith stood frozen on the spot as Mary majestically walked across the room and embraced Mandy.

Steve stood perfectly still; he was as rigid as a statue. It was as though Mary had cast a spell over him and had turned by magic to stone. He was speechless; he was stunned and he was confused. Mary's stance and action against him had taken him by complete surprise.

He had not expected anyone to oppose him, least of all Mary! His five feet tall bespectacled and very delicately framed wife, a woman who in all the very many years that I had known her, I cannot remember her ever having spoken a sentence.

My very slim but educated gamble, was that when the crunch came and the happiness of her children mattered the most, that she would oppose her ogre of a husband. And she proved me right!

With her few barely audible words of comfort and kindness to our family, he was thrown completely off balance and the expression on his contorted dazed face showed it too!

Mary had hit him so hard on the chin with a knockout punch that was timed to perfection, that Smith's fight was over!

His huge arms flayed, he tried to speak, but no words would come out of his quivering lips, instead he gulped for air. His face turned as bright red as a red-hot poker, his fists were clenched and shaking and he ran out of the room thoroughly humiliated. Just like the leadership battle that had just failed, his exit from the room turned into a farce!

As he ran in fright away from the crowd that now opposed him, he stumbled over his own shoes and sent a small table of teacups flying! As he disappeared running away from our house the children, women and men in the room burst into shouts of joy and whoops of cheering and dancing!

Our victory was now assured!

Big Steve Smith, the hard drinking, hard swearing, ex-weightlifter of a monster, had done all the hard work for me. He had succeeded in uniting every person present, into a force for good instead of a force for evil!

Everyone in our living room that night was from that moment onwards welded together as best friends forever!

And what happened next was truly remarkable!

CHAPTER 23
TRUE LOVE CONQUERS ALL

My first overriding thoughts after Steve had stormed out of our house were to comfort his timid little wife Mary.

Mary stood no taller than five feet in her highest shoes and she was as thin as a butcher's pencil, aged around forty with shining grey hair and wire-rimmed glasses. She was small, incredibly quiet and frail-looking.

I walked over to her and asked her if she was OK.

To my amazement, instead of being shaken, she was totally calm. "I am fine, Paul," she said and please forgive Steven. He is having one of his childish tantrums; he often gets them when he does not get his own way. It will take time for him to calm down, it could be as much as two months before he talks to me again, but he will not lift a finger against me!

"If he ever did physically attack me, I would leave him for good and he knows that and the loneliness and guilt would kill him. I am the mother of his two daughters that come riding here, Paul, and he loves them, but he cannot find the words to say the right things. He does try, but usually he ends up making a mess of a situation.

"I am so sorry for his behaviour here tonight, all of us here knew it was coming and for these past few years it has been boiling up inside of him. I am sorry, but he says the most stupid things at times without deeply thinking about what he is saying or thinking of the feelings of the people he says things to.

"So from me, Paul, please do forgive him for what he just did!"

I was stunned by Mary's serenity, logical explanation and deep thought for Mandy, our children and for me, she really was everything that her husband was not; she was sincere, delicate, kind and caring, and in all the years that I had known her, I realised that I had not known the woman at all.

Normally she was so shy, timid and meek; she had always been a lady of very few words. Now I saw her in a completely different light. Behind the closed doors of her own home I suddenly became fully aware that it was Mary who wore the trousers in her house and it was not the loutish oaf that she had of a husband!

And it was this fact that I had banked on, in my gambling strategy. By enticing Steve to speak his mind in the brutish way that he had done, he had unwittingly played straight into my hands. And he had made Mary into the hero that she really was!

So I took her hands in mine and thanked her from the bottom of my heart for her brave speech and kind thoughts for my family and for me.

To which she humbly and simply replied, "Thank you, Paul," then lowered her head and resumed her usual calm demure posture.

At that moment the group in the room who had listened and watched Mary and I, erupted with more cheers and applause and for a minute or more, I stood still and let the warmth of the crowd wash over me.

It was then that I became aware just how much Mandy, the boys and I were loved by our genuine true friends. The sensation that we were loved moved Mandy and I both to tears.

I believe the emotions, the tensions and the worries that were built up inside us burst their river banks, and the tears of joy flowed!

After a few moments of complete sobbing and breakdown in front of the gathered assembly, I dried my eyes and thanked everyone from the bottom of our hearts for their support.

I told them, frankly and honestly, that the members of the Wimblington Riding Club had shown great courage and solidarity and that I needed just one kind favour to see us all safely sorted, once and for all.

Basically I told them that I needed each man, woman and child to accompany me and Mandy the next morning at 9 am sharp, in a visit to see Jan Limming at her Peterborough solicitors' office. And I asked them all, "Please would they do that for the sake of our family and also do that for the future of the Wimblington Riding Club, which means so much to us all!"

Without exception, everyone said that they would attend!

Then I telephoned Jan that evening at her private home number and made her aware that we would all be on our way to see her the following day.

Bright and early at 8 am the next morning, a fleet of cars assembled once again in our driveway.

Mandy and I humbly thanked the parents for attending and our sons played in the sunshine with the other boys and girls, who were all ecstatic at having a full day off school.

Precisely, one hour later at nine o'clock we were standing on the front doorstep to Jan's office waiting for her to unbolt the giant red-painted office front door.

"Welcome and do come in," she beamed, and she led us all upstairs to the massive first floor directors' boardroom.

"Right," she barked into her intercom, "Joyce, I want you please to bring teas, coffees and lemonade and plenty of biscuits too. Oh and Joyce, do come in as fast as you can with your notepad and pen, as we need to take down some very important information!"

Joyce, her elderly assistant, appeared almost immediately looking rather like a Mary Poppins, very straight-backed, hair in a bun, high collar blouse, pushing mid-sixties and Jan's favourite secretary. And if she had just left Dick Van-Dyke on the rooftops to the office, I would have not been in the very least surprised.

Jan asked Joyce kindly and politely, "Joyce? Please take down the name and addresses of every person in the room and note that they are all members of the Wimblington Riding Club. Make a careful note which person is a committee member, who the club secretary is, who the chairperson is and who the vice chairperson is and so on."

Then Jan addressed the room. "Oh and by the way everyone, are there any members of the club that are not present this morning?"

To which we all tried to speak at once, which was quite amusing.

"Only one person is not present, Jan," I ventured. "That is a Mr Steven Smith, he is just an ordinary member, but his wife, Mary, and his two fine daughters, Sally and Susan, are here in his stead."

To which Mary and her daughters all arose from the table and the girls gave Jan a very polite curtsey.

"Excellent," Jan exclaimed. "Now let us proceed with business!"

One hour later, by 10 am exactly we were finished.

Then Jan announced, "Ladies and gentlemen, on behalf of my solicitors' practice of which I am the senior partner, I would like to thank each of you for attending today. I want you all to know that the statements that you have given me confirms that the Wimblington Riding Club relinquishes all rights and claims to the title of Paul and Mandy's property, and I will inform the Kingston Building Society of this fact.

"I am now totally confident that the transaction will be concluded this morning. So my suggestion to you all is that you should return to Paul and Mandy's house, to enjoy the sunshine and the rest of the day together. And it is my very strong suggestion that you should celebrate this momentous and wonderful occasion!"

And thanking Jan for her kindness and hospitality, that is exactly what we all did!

By the middle of the day the barbeque was going and the party was in full swing. The children were running around the garden like wild things. The drinks were flowing and the music played and the members of the riding club were having a ball!

Then the telephone rang and William, my eldest twin, came and called me to it. It was Jan!

"I just thought you should know that it's done," she said. "Your house is now owned by you again! And Paul, well done, I always knew that you could do it!"

And for the second time in only two days the tears filled my eyes and I cried like a newborn baby!

"Oh," she continued, "do give my love please to Mandy, your boys and to all your excellent friends that you have and do have a great celebration on me!"

And with that, she was gone.

The words were choked in the back of my throat and the tears ran down my face, and so quietly you could hardly make out the sound that I whispered in the telephone, I said, "Thank you, Jan!"

So it was that since January 8th 1990 with the collapse of Chancery Bank in London up to that present time, over five and a half years later, that I had suffered immense human cruelty.

Now at long last it was over! Our home was now our own once more! And our friends of the Wimblington Riding Club were now cast iron friends forever! Even Steven Smith was welcome as a friend!

All those years, from January 1990 to 1995, I had endured enormous personal grief and hardship and yet I had discovered a wealth of beautiful genuine love that I never knew existed.

Jan Limming, truly loved me as a human being.

Every man woman and child, apart from Steve Smith, in the Wimblington Riding Club loved Mandy, my sons and me.

Even Peter Reeve had shown us true love and kindness, because the man who had never arranged a mortgage before in his life could very simply have said to me and Mandy, "Sorry guys, I am not a mortgage broker, I cannot help you." But he did not do that, no, he pulled off a miracle when even I, the eternal optimist, had privately given up all hope!

And who proved to be the greatest supporter and true love of all? As always, it was Mandy! She was the true heroine of the whole tragic story. Through all the many years of financial and terrible emotional pain that I suffered, it was Mandy that kept me sane.

In fact I know for certain that it was her deep true love for me, and her support when I needed it most, that kept me alive and kept me from literally going insane!

I am eternally in her debt!

And despite all the nastiness and cruelty was thrust upon me, an innocent customer of a London bank that collapsed, nobody could take the love that we had away!

It was then following the repurchase of our home that I realised that genuine true love and true friendship really does conquer all!

CHAPTER 24
BEGINNING AGAIN – THE ADVENTURE
CONTINUES
"FROM ZERO TO HERO!"

The repurchase of our home was one of the finest achievements that I ever had in my entire life! At that time we were still poor but at last we had a secure roof over our heads.

To thank all our genuine and real friends from the Wimblington Riding Club, Mandy and I found silver trophies at our very own Sunday car boot sales that I opened from the mid 1990s onwards and these we donated to the club, so that the children could have fun and compete for them at their annual shows. We also held garden parties on the anniversary of the day that we purchased back our home and we still hold these each and every year to this very day, because there is absolutely no way that we will ever forget the true kindness shown to us by our very close friends!

We made a solemn vow to our riding club, that no matter what the circumstances were in the future and despite now not having anything in writing, that the club was safe and was here to stay for all time!

Twelve months after that time in history in late 1996, I did return to enormous wealth, and again, I started from absolutely nothing.

In my next book *From Zero to Hero* I will tell you exactly how I did it! How I had to confront and rise above all the misery, poverty, pain and adversity contained within this true book.

I will explain for you in graphic detail exactly how I made my next amazing fortune.

Oh and then in my third book: *Success My Way* I will also tell you precisely in intimate detail how again, from absolutely nothing, I made the £200 million pound fortune contained in this true book too, because so far you have only learnt what happened to me when a London bank collapsed on me. You have yet to learn exactly how I made and built up my first vast fortune.

Study books two and three and you will discover the reason why it is that they have been written in that sequence and if you think that is exciting, there are three books in all in my real life story sequence!

By the time you have studied all three you will learn what makes a great fighter tick, and you will learn how to survive in the real world, as a self-made businessman or businesswoman. I will teach you everything that I know and it will surprise you.

If you truly want to be a self-made business tycoon and warrior, then read and learn how it is done. You need no education, no posh birth and no money to start with. All you need is the knowledge that I will give to you!

So if you want to create a fortune of your own from absolutely nothing and you want to learn how to survive in the real world of business, do not miss my exciting true books.

Learn from me how you can do it too, and then go out and make a fortune for yourself! And remember, that if a poor little boy like me from the bleak and sparsely populated, wild and wind-strewn, flat lands of the Fens of Cambridgeshire can do it, then you can do it too!

Oh! If you think I asked my father for one penny, you would be wrong. That is something that I would never do! I have always been self-made and independent!

It is true that Gerald and I did respect each other as self made business tycoons, but as you will later discover we did not enjoy a close loving father and son relationship!

Pity! But there you are!

I guess that was because we were two determined, dynamic people, that we simply clashed, most of the time!

CHAPTER 25
THE INNOCENT MUST BE PROTECTED

Now that you have read my true nightmare story, you will have come to realise that this book is far more than the retelling of a very tragic story! It is more than learning some tale of something that happened to one guy and his family. No, this book is far more than that! It is a warning! It is essentially two things: first it is a wake-up call for all the victims of all the banks that will collapse! And, second: it is the beginning of a crusade. To change the laws in both the UK and in every so-called civilised society in the world, because the innocent must be 100% protected and 100% compensated when banks go bust!

I was *attacked and left for dead,* I was abandoned by the Thatcher government of the time, but do not be mistaken, today in 2012 nothing has changed. There still are no laws that force today's governments to give you 100% protection and there are no laws either that force any governments anywhere in the world to give you 100% compensation either when banks go bust, which in the highly volatile world that we live in today is far more likely to happen than it was during the time of my true story!

So now is the time for change! Now you, the innocent, have the biggest opportunity in your lives to see that you, your wife, your children, your homes, your live savings, and everything else that you hold most dear, are protected.

With the explosive state that the world's economies are actually in, now is the time to that the innocent must be protected. Not just in the UK but in every country throughout the world. And there is no earthly reason why the innocent cannot be protected by the passing of new laws.

OK, as a rational human being I accept that the world is, and will never be, a perfect place. Small companies do go bust every day and that cannot be stopped.

Big companies do go bust quite often and that cannot be avoided either. Banks still get in financial trouble and it is not always their own fault and countries do fall into recession and, sadly, mankind has not yet managed to avoid that fact either.

These are facts of life that we must accept when we live in a world where there exists many separately functioning free-market economies, where people, companies and governments freely exchange goods, products and services with one another every day.

As result of this, the world is and never will be a perfect place. But I say this, the world can and it must become a safer place.

Because what I do not accept, is the absence of caution, as a very successful self-made businessman I state that it is the lack of caution that is the biggest factor that kills companies of any size and it kills banks and it kills whole countries too!

In 2012 in a truly global economy, there has never been a more important time for international caution because when caution is abandoned the system at all levels of life fails!

To stop the misery that was caused to me and my family and the 10,000 other poor souls that my companies fed from happening again all that is needed are two things:

First: the law in every country of the world must be changed. Governments of the world must be forced by you, the innocent, to protect and to compensate you! Governments must *guarantee you* 100% protect and 100% compensation when banks go bust!

And secondly: so as to protect themselves from banks getting in serious trouble in the first place, every government must regulate their banking sector to a far tighter degree than ever before!

Also I am sorry, but the days of the bosses of the banks writing themselves millions of pounds of wages and bonuses has to stop! Instead they must become caring and thoughtful for the smallest of their customers. Because it is the millions of small guys who support and maintain the whole system! And they are essential to protect!

Taking the United Kingdom as an example, the Bank of England as the watchdog and regulator for the British banks, must have much more power and they must intervene more in the way that the British banks are run so that they can strictly demand caution!

And if every country in the world does the same, then the collapse of banks or the need to bail them out with billions of pounds of public money will be avoided.

Only then can the total devastation that collapsed banks leave behind them be stopped and the chronic human misery that they thrust upon their innocent customers can become a thing of the past.

Make no mistake about it, immediate action and a change in the laws of the world has to take place and take place now!

You have only got to remind yourself of:

1. The collapse of the Irish economy in 2010.
2. The collapse of the North American real estate market of the same time.
3. The enormous financial support that had to be given to rescue the several banks and building societies in

Great Britain, including Northern Rock and the Royal Bank of Scotland, among others.

4. The collapse of the banks and the economy in recent times in Iceland!

5. And of course the collapse of the three banks featured in this true book.

6. The collapse of the economies in Greece, Portugal and Spain in the Eurozone.

7. The chronic economic condition of many countries in the world today.

And tragically these are but a few examples and the underlying reason in the failure in every case above is human error that is caused by the lack of tighter regulation and the absence of caution!

Without a doubt in 2012 and, in all the years to come, everyone on this earth must learn that there are not one but that there are two big C's that kill people: one C is Cancer, and we must find a cure for it. The other big C is Caution and we must find a cure for that too!

Because both are killers and so my crusade to change the world that we live in has begun with the publication of this book. Who will join me to make the world a safer place in which we can all live?

I now invite you all now to contact me at:

paulgsalter@hotmail.co.uk

I await you email with excitement. Let us campaign for world that has stability and let us demand the introduction of *100% protection and 100% compensation laws for the protection of the innocent!*

Because the world can and must become a safer place in which we can all live!

My final words on leaving this tragic and true story are this:

I pray that what happened to me and my family is never allowed to happen to anyone on this planet, ever again!

Let us fight together for new laws that give *100% guaranteed protection and 100% compensation rights for the innocent.*

This applies to every one of every nation, no matter what you religion is. No matter what the colour of your skin is. Because unless you act now to protect yourselves, you are in deeply serious trouble!

Every government in the world must be forced by new laws to regulate their banks to a far greater degree than ever before, for the protection and preservation of mankind!

We, the innocent of the world, must fight to see that banks that go bust are a fact of the past and not a fact of our future!

Join me now, fight for your freedom, fight for justice and fight for your basic human right of protection and compensation. Demand action now from the ones that you elect to serve you and demand that they protect you!

And let us make *100% protection and 100% compensation laws your Basic Human Right!*

Fight for a better an6d safer world in which we and our children and their children too, can live in peace! Because until new laws force governments *to 100% protect and to 100% compensate the innocent are passed in every country in the world.*

Until then, no one in the world is safe!

Do you feel safe right now?

You do!

Then you really are a fool!